What To Expect
When Parenting
Children With **ADHD**

A 9-step plan to master the struggles and
triumphs of parenting a child with ADHD

by PENNY WILLIAMS

Grace-Everett Press

D1279229

For my family:
baby daddy, Mr. T;
beauty, Warrior Girl;
and wild child, Ricochet.

Look what Momma did! I turned all that obsessing about ADHD and learning disabilities into a book to help other parents and families like us. I couldn't have done it without your strength and love fueling me.

In memory of Tanji Dewberry, friend, fellow Warrior Mom, and author of "Oh Fiddlesticks," a children's book inspired by her son who had ADHD. Tanji knew I had books within me and encouraged me often. She is deeply missed.

Table of Contents

Foreword

As anyone reading this book probably already knows, being the parent of a child with ADHD is no frolic in the park.

The disorder affects all sorts of children, including kids with high intelligence, potential, and good hearts. All too often, however, it can bring out the worst in children and their families, feeding anxiety, depression, and oppositional behavior. Marriages may falter. Siblings may rebel. Mothers, in particular, may feel besieged by constant crises and judgment from teachers and other parents who don't have a clue of the difficulties we face.

As Penny Williams so obviously knows, you and your child will have the best chance of surviving — and maybe, just maybe, even thriving — if you can find the resilience to educate yourself, reach out to others in the same boat, and morph from an anxious, overwhelmed mom to a positive and confident Warrior Mom. This is clearly the spirit in which Penny has mothered Ricochet, all the while providing comfort and encouragement to so many other mothers in need through her previous book, *Boy Without Instructions*, blogging, and her reporting for outlets such as *ADDitude Magazine*.

I admire Penny tremendously. As I read *What to Expect When Parenting a Child with ADHD*, I suspected that it would have helped make me a better mother, had I had such a book, say, ten years ago. (Sigh.) I particularly appreciate the fact that Penny has no ax to grind; the information she offers on these pages is non-biased and well-founded in research. She has certainly done her homework.

Having a whopper of a case of ADHD myself, on all too many days I ended up as a surrendered mom, rather than a Warrior Mom. I'm pretty sure the only reason I've muddled through sans major catastrophes (knock on wood) — including traffic accidents, stints in juvenile hall, drug addictions, or teen pregnancies — is because of the priceless comfort and good advice I've found in friendships with other mothers of challenging kids. When I was in the thick of parenting my son, Buzz, who was diagnosed at age nine with both ADHD and Oppositional Defiant Disorder (ODD), there were no books that offered this spirit of informed and helpful friendship to the world, which is why I wrote my own.

Now, through Penny's dedicated work — particularly her sage, upbeat advice on everything from how to write a letter to a teacher to introduce your child, to how to increase protein-rich foods in your child's diet, to how to discern the authentic line between "I can't" and "I won't" — we can all tap into a much larger, more powerful, hard-knocks knowledgeable network of mothers helping mothers. Because behind every surviving Buzz and Ricochet, as you might guess, there's a woman who has made it her nearly full-time job to support their health, happiness, and success. Penny's book offers you company, consolation, information, and entertainment as you embark on that journey. Read it and re-read it, and enjoy the ride!

Katherine Ellison

Pulitzer Prize-winning journalist, author, consultant, and public speaker

Author of *Buzz: A Year of Paying Attention* and Co-Author of *Loving Learning: How Progressive Education Can Save America's Schools*

I am one of you.

Finding out your child has ADHD is life-altering. It changes all you thought you knew about parenting and about your child. Most people only know the "facts" of the court of public opinion until ADHD becomes part of their lives, through family member, friend, or even co-worker. Then they're forced to discover the real truth, but only if they're open to accepting that ADHD is truly a disability — a neurological condition that limits a person's ability to meet all expectations of "normalcy."

When my son was diagnosed with ADHD at the age of six in November, 2008, I didn't know a thing about the disorder. I believed that ADHD was real and was a challenge for those who had it, but like many, I also believed that medication for ADHD was merely "drugging a child into submission." I was truly ignorant on this subject!

The contrast between expectations and capability is stark but invisible.

Fortunately, my first instinct after Ricochet's diagnosis was to learn all I could about ADHD. I immediately checked out a stack of books from the library and parked myself in front of the computer to search the Internet tirelessly until I had a handle on parenting my special needs child. I spent more than two years in that obsessed-with-making-it-better state, discovering new information or potential treatments, trying these new discoveries with my son, getting high on hope, and then, usually, crashing onto the jagged rocks of utter disappointment.

The behavioral doctor told me little about ADHD the day he declared those dreaded three words, "Ricochet has ADHD." He gave me four or five single-page handouts and then wanted to write a prescription for stimulant medication often prescribed to treat ADHD. I was paralyzed by shock and fear — I refused the prescription that day on the grounds that I had to discuss it with my husband, Mr. T, which I immediately did. I couldn't dial my phone fast enough as Ricochet and I fled the scene of the destruction of all I thought I knew about my child, and my parenting.

I was thrust back out into the world with some generic fact sheets, those three ugly words echoing in my head, and this sweet, smart little boy — who kept getting into trouble and couldn't succeed in school — bouncing along by my side. No direction. No instructions. Just a diagnosis of a four letter acronym branded on my child for all eternity — that's how I felt during those initial moments, at least. I rushed home to grieve, holed up in my bedroom for three days.

After the initial shock mellowed, I tackled it like a ~~crazy person~~ warrior though. I spent hours every single day researching ADHD and communicating with other parents of children with ADHD. I taught myself what I needed to know and got to know my son more meaningfully through trial-and-error-style parenting. I look back now, six years later, and I see how much simpler learning to parent my child with ADHD could have been had I just been given a guide book, some instructions, or even some general direction. It certainly wouldn't have taken two years to learn how to parent my child in light of his disorder if I hadn't been left entirely to fend for myself.

But that's exactly what it's like for most parents once their child is diagnosed with ADHD. Their world has ~~imploded~~ been turned upside down with no guidance on how to create order. An ADHD diagnosis is ambiguous and downright scary.

You are not alone though! There are hundreds of thousands of parents *just like you* who have found themselves paralyzed with fear when their child was diagnosed with ADHD. I know, because **I am one of them**. There's a definitive learning curve to this special parenthood, and it takes time to get to the top of the curve — as I said, it took me more than two long years. I'm sharing what I learned on my long travels on this learning curve with the hope that it will shorten your journey. Don't expect to have everything under control with your child at home and school, with treatment, and in building all their lagging skills quickly or all at once. Parenting a child with ADHD is a marathon, not a sprint. It takes preparation, dogged determination, and time (and for some, possibly, lots of wine).

Use this book as a life-preserver while you learn how to swim and navigate the waters of ADHD. Soon you'll begin to tread water without thinking about it. Yeah, there are a lot of books on ADHD out there already — but there isn't one that I know of that brings all aspects of parenting a child with ADHD together and tells it like it really is strictly from a parent's perspective, but with optimism. I promise, I'm *keeping it real* about parenting a child with ADHD.

Good luck on your new journey, Warrior Parent. May the strength of calm, understanding, and empathy be with you!

Penny

P.S. — I mention a lot of personal experiences in this book, but I don't typically reveal the entire story here, because this book is more than a book of my experiences. However, you can pick up my previous book, *Boy Without Instructions: Surviving the Learning Curve of Parenting a Child with ADHD*, and read all the tragedies and triumphs referenced here and many other stories of transforming from a grief-stricken, obsessed-with-ADHD control-freak and helicopter mom to an optimistic and (mostly) confident parent of a child who happens to have ADHD.

P.P.S. — I must be *clear*. I am not an expert in the field of ADHD in any way except through the trial-by-fire of raising a boy with ADHD. The advice you will glean from this book is a culmination of recommendations I've gathered from the professionals in our lives, through reading and researching reputable sources, and through my own experiences parenting my son, Ricochet. Always seek the guidance of ADHD professionals before implementing any ADHD treatment for your child.

My New Parenthood

When you set out to have children, you wish for a healthy and happy baby. You may hope for a girl or hope for a boy, but you know either is great as long as it is healthy. While you may have fleeting fears of illness or disability during pregnancy, you plan for a "normal" child unless someone tells you otherwise.

I, of course, was no different. With my first pregnancy, I was desperate to have a girl. I do mean *desperate!* I didn't have experience with little boys. This pacifist Momma didn't have any interest in revving engines, guns, or explosives. I had an unhealthy fear that I would not know what to do with a boy. I knew I'd love my child, boy or girl, but I was truly desperate for a girl. I had a few issues during pregnancy, but my beautiful daughter, Warrior Girl, was full-term and healthy. All ten fingers, all ten toes, and a great set of lungs — a totally "normal" little girl. She had some challenges, like colic, but being her momma came naturally for the most part.

Three years later, I found myself pregnant again. I wasn't so desperate to have a girl this time, although I still had no idea what to do with a boy. Long before my first ultrasound, I knew I was carrying a boy. All that extra testosterone has no place in a woman's body! I had a teenager's acne, I was so zapped my knuckles nearly dragged the floor, and I had heartburn that had me sitting up to sleep for the last six months of pregnancy! His birth was prolonged and difficult. Definitely a boy! He was already ~~wreaking havoc~~ turning my world upside down.

But he was a beautiful, healthy baby boy, and he loves his momma like only a son can. Through his toddler and pre-k years, we never noticed anything more than age-appropriate, little boy behavior. Nothing that was out of the ordinary for a child that age. Nothing that was cause for any sort of concern. Being the momma I knew how to be was still applicable and working well for our family.

It all fell apart when Ricochet started kindergarten though. He was the proverbial square peg in a round hole. Ricochet was trying to fit, but just couldn't. He was too active for the classroom; he didn't treat scissors with the caution they demand; he couldn't write his name legibly; he liked to talk at inappropriate times; he had zero interest in reading. These all should have been red flags. Hell, they were red flags flying frantically right in front of my face, but we all missed them. His charter school teacher frequently pointed her finger at us and our home life, and said we just hadn't prepared him for kindergarten and we should have waited another year to enroll him. But we recognized how super smart he is and that we are great parents — we knew that wasn't the source of his problems in school.

I was certain it was the kindergarten environment, or the teacher, or the loose culture of the charter school, but not a problem with my sweet, intelligent boy. We enrolled Ricochet in a mainstream public school the following year for first grade. I was confident Ricochet would hit his stride and everything would be great in the new school. But just a couple of weeks in, I noticed a pattern of bad behavior reports coming home again. Finally, I saw the red flag. I felt it in the sinking feeling in my gut, too. That proved it wasn't the kindergarten classroom environment and it wasn't the kindergarten teacher. Something was going on with Ricochet.

My son was diagnosed with ADHD on November 24, 2008. One single day that changed each life in our family. And yet it wasn't one single day. It isn't one single day. It's every day of our lives. Every day of **his** life.

His diagnosis was a complete shock. I had been researching all sorts of learning disabilities for a few months by then. I knew there was something wrong, something different. I knew my son had a learning disability, and I just had to figure out which one and get him the help he needed. I checked out half a dozen or more books at a time from the library, but I always skimmed the chapters on ADHD. ADHD was not my son.

But that November day came and defied all I thought I knew. Life is never what you expect.

The doctor's office was big and intimidating and scary that day. There were giant leaf sculptures hanging from the ceiling and cute bugs painted on the walls, bright colors all around, and big windows to let the sunshine in. It was designed to put children at ease, but it was cavernous too, and I felt as though I was about to be swallowed up. The decor had no effect on the purpose of the day. I'd come to this place to find out what was wrong with my son. Ironically, this was an ominous, frightening place for the grown-ups who never imagined themselves in such a place.

I sat on the edge of my chair in the waiting room; I couldn't lean back as that would require me to relax my muscles. I clutched my purse and my paperwork tight against my chest. I studied my fingernails and the linear pattern on the floor. Eye contact with the other parents was not an option that day. I didn't know how I related to those parents just yet. I couldn't let them in just yet.

It was just Ricochet and I at the doctor's office that day. I had prepared myself and knew what to expect. There wouldn't be any decisions to be made. The doctor would talk and play with Ricochet, give me a diagnosis, maybe explain a bit about it and how to treat it — I'd have the information to give to the school, and we would be armed with the knowledge to help Ricochet.

I told myself to be prepared for any diagnosis, as long as it was accurate. A diagnosis would be the first step to knowing how to help Ricochet function successfully in school with whatever this current obstacle was. I told myself I could even handle ADHD, as it's treatable.

Once the doctor said those three words, "Ricochet has ADHD," I completely checked out.

{Hello? Anybody home?}

It turns out I was not prepared. My mind was a jumbled mess. I could no longer follow what the doctor was saying to me. It was muffled sounds, and I couldn't make sense of it. My mind was racing, trying to rationalize what I'd just been told. I thought back to what I had read of ADHD. I thought about how it would tragically alter his life forever. I thought about how school was always going to be nearly impossible for him. I thought about how he was always going to be sad and feel inferior. I thought about how I had to keep myself together and not cry in front of this stranger, this matter-of-fact doctor. I held my breath and wished for time to stand still.

Thankfully, time didn't stand still that day. The doctor went on explaining ADHD to deaf ears and told me he wanted to prescribe a stimulant medication. Somehow, I heard that very clearly as the sound of a gong; it jolted me right back to the present. I was one of the ADHD-ignorant people who feared medication. I told the doctor I couldn't make that decision without talking to my husband, but I wasn't ready to make that decision after just two minutes to process my son having a neurological disorder either. I nodded a lot and got the heck out of there.

I remember this blur so vividly. I can't remember the details of the conversation, but I can still feel the emotions of those moments.

I wanted to fall apart, and I allowed myself to grieve for a few days. Mr. T and I discussed the diagnosis and the recommended treatment. In our ignorance, we talked that night about how we didn't want to "dope" our child. But we also took a step back and told ourselves anything was worth a try for our son's happiness. If the medication created a zombie, or any other unwanted side effects, we'd discontinue use and look for other options. I am so grateful that we could achieve that perspective and make a rational, goal-oriented plan. While falling apart in this sort of situation feels warranted, it doesn't accomplish a thing. Getting beyond what is "wrong" with my son, educating myself, and advocating for his success and happiness has been a sort of treatment in itself. Knowing what we are facing removes the fear. (And the medication works wonders for his achievement in school, too.)

I am not sure how I overlooked ADHD as a possible diagnosis for Ricochet. Denial, I guess. The signs were everywhere. From the long, difficult labor, the extra hours on Pitocin, the delay in baby milestones, the sudden talkativeness, the difficulty controlling his body, the lack of focus in a busy classroom full of new activities to explore, the unmanageable behavior from a very sweet and kind kid... The signs really were everywhere, but I didn't know enough about ADHD to connect the dots. Each instance by itself can be something entirely different. But, dots connected, it is a clear picture of ADHD. It's a clear picture of my son.

So there I was, thrust into a new parenthood. A world of doctor's appointments, behavioral therapy, occupational therapy, daily medications, teacher conferences, special education laws, school accommodations, different nutrition, guilt, anxiety, and even grief. I hadn't had any training for this motherhood, and it didn't come so naturally. I didn't expect it nor, frankly, did I even want it. But this job, this new motherhood, came with Ricochet, and I certainly wouldn't reject him.

Parenting a child with ADHD is indisputably more difficult and downright exhausting. There are so many more appointments, so many more worries, so much more stress. But there's also so much more strength, courage, resilience, determination, and simple gratitude for the small stuff, because everything a child with ADHD does they do very big.

My new parenthood can be tricky and downright exhausting, but it's made me a stronger, better person, and I'm certainly grateful for that.

It is time to get prepared for your new parenthood, too. Parenting a child with ADHD is trial-by-fire with very sweet rewards when you learn to control the flames.

"Everybody is a genius. But if you judge a fish by its ability to climb a tree, it will live its whole life believing that it is stupid."
- Albert Einstein

Step 1: Get Over It

›››››››››››

> "Sometimes people let the same problem make them miserable
> for years when they could just say, 'So what.' That's one of my
> favorite things to say. So what."
>   —Andy Warhol, *The Philosophy of Andy Warhol*

Let's face it. You weren't expecting ADHD. No one does. It comes at you suddenly, from behind, and with great force. It's more than being blindsided; it's like falling out of the boat, without a lifejacket, and without knowing how to swim. *Oh, by the way, there are piranhas under that dark surface, too.* It's unexpected and terrifying.

So what do you do when you're *not* expecting ADHD?

Freak out!

Go ahead. I'm not kidding. Freak out! Panic! Have a pity party.

Feel sorry for yourself, your child, and your family — it's natural. Take some time to wallow in the fact that your in-utero plans for your child's future have possibly changed altogether. I know ~~you regret buying this book now~~ that's not the advice you expected, but you have to acknowledge and validate

1

those feelings of fear and sadness so you can move beyond the shock and grief and eventually reach a good place. Acceptance is key to effective parenting.

When you've cried until there are no more tears, and taken in the "Why me?" monster as though he is your new BFF, come back and pick up this book again to discover your next steps to get on your way to *successfully* parenting a child with ADHD. Take as long as you need — there aren't rules for this, and I'll wait until you're ready.

First Things First

Okay, stop ~~losing it~~ panicking now. While it feels like it initially, an ADHD diagnosis is nothing to panic about. In fact, I challenge you to celebrate the impending clarity that comes with diagnosis. There's a certain amount of relief to finally knowing why your child is struggling.

There is one essential thing to remember when your child is first diagnosed with ADHD — *you are not alone.* Say it with me, "I am not alone. I am not the only parent who struggles with this special brand of parenting." You may even want to post it on your bathroom mirror and treat it like a personal affirmation for a while. It certainly won't hurt. Parenting a child with special needs can be very isolating, so you will need to consistently remind yourself that others know a similar journey. There's safety in numbers, as they say.

> I am not alone. I am not the only parent who struggles with this special brand of parenting.

Acceptance of your child, just the way he or she is, is crucial, now more than ever.

Grieve the Loss

I'm sure you visualized your child gloating about their latest A, or crossing the stage during college graduation, at some point during your pregnancy or adoption process. It's an innate instinct to want ~~to raise the next Bill Gates~~ the very best for our children and to visualize their life's milestones very early.

An ADHD diagnosis often initially feels like an abrupt end of many of your dreams for your child. Finding out your child has ADHD establishes the possibility that all **your** dreams for them may not come true. But it doesn't mean **their** dreams aren't possible. Put your dreams for them aside and focus on their strengths and what those strengths offer your child as they are championed.

Let's face it, receiving an ADHD diagnosis for your child is ~~earth-shattering~~ tough. No, it's not a terminal illness or a physical handicap, but that doesn't mean you shouldn't feel sad and grieve. You've been blindsided — your pain is real and valid, even if it isn't as intense as someone else's. You just found out your child has a neurological disorder — that something didn't quite go right when his or her brain was developing — and that entitles you to a period of sorrow. If you weren't upset about it, *that* would be something to worry about.

It's natural to grieve when your child is diagnosed with any disability. Your world has changed — either your expectations have been shattered, or you have come to the realization that the ~~madness~~ chaos is here to stay, at least somewhat. While it's necessary to go through that period of grief, you also have to move forward and get beyond it. Feeling sorry long term doesn't help the situation one bit.

> *Finding out your child has ADHD establishes the possibility that all your dreams for them may not come true. But it doesn't mean their dreams aren't possible.*

Take a little time to be sad, angry, scared, heartbroken... Sit in a room alone for a couple of days. Take a bubble bath until you shrivel. Cry. Scream. Recoil. It's okay to be irrational for a few moments and let these feelings surface.

It's even healthy, dare I say. Take a few days, maybe a week, to process and work through your feelings about your child having ADHD — then move on because wallowing is not going to help you or your child.

> *Cry. Scream. Recoil. It's okay to be irrational for a few moments and let these feelings surface.*

I sat in front of the TV alone in my bedroom and stared out the window for a couple of days after my son's diagnosis. I cried a lot, and I have a faint memory of eating lots of ice cream. I tried not to think about ADHD, yet it was all I thought about for days. Years, in fact, if I'm honest with myself.

Gratitude and positivity are the only roads to *genuine* happiness. For that is how we survive, and eventually thrive. It is easy to feel hopeless when parenting a special needs child. It takes fortitude and a survivor's will to move beyond it objectively and live in a place of optimism. I decided wallowing in my sorrow wasn't doing me, Ricochet, or anyone else in my family any good (not even the dog). Denial and tears were not going to erase Ricochet's ADHD, and they weren't going to teach Mr. T and me how to do the best for him either.

So I chose to direct my compass toward the positive and left grief for what I cannot change behind. Do I still have pangs of grief some days? Sure. But I don't let it consume me. I adjust my compass back toward the positive as soon as possible.

Next, I moved on to gathering knowledge, the next crucial step in successfully parenting a child with ADHD.

Learn the Facts

The only hope we have of conquering ADHD — thriving in spite of it — is to understand it, as much as one can comprehend ADHD anyway. You must learn all you can about this disability, this different ability, this ADHD.

There are many free resources for gathering knowledge in this millennium. If you live in a bigger city, you will likely have access to many books on ADHD in your local library. In smaller cities like mine, there may only be a couple of titles available to borrow on the subject.

The Internet is also a vast resource of knowledge. Be careful when researching ADHD online though; there are a lot of skeptics and snake-oil pushers penetrating the online ADHD communities. When researching ADHD on the Internet, be sure to carefully consider the source of the information. Some credible sites for ADHD information include: Healthline, WebMD, CHADD, NIMH, Mayo Clinic, NCLD, PsychCentral, and ADDitudeMag.

Of course, there are dozens and dozens of titles on ADHD available in bookstores too, if you're up for purchasing the information. Some reputable authors on the subject include: Dr. Edward Hallowell, Dr. Russell Barkley, Dr. Ross Greene, Dr. Patricia Quinn, Vincent J. Monstra, James Forgan, Nancy Ratey, Peg Dawson, Katherine Ellison, and many more…

The "ADHD Guides" that your doctor likely suggested you read when your child was diagnosed are all about the diagnostic criteria, the symptoms, and all the negative characteristics of ADHD. These books are scientific medical writings on "ADHD the Disability." The only thing I first gleaned from the "ADHD Guides" was how my son couldn't control his behavior, would not be able to sit still, would always struggle with organization, would essentially live a chaotic, out-of-(his)-control life. That was not a good message to start my journey with.

But I am Momma. I was not giving up that easily. It is my job to prepare a path to success and happiness for my children. It's a good thing I didn't give up on gathering knowledge about ADHD after reading the "guides" because I would have missed the good stuff.

I advise you to limit the "ADHD Guide" type books to only a few, at least at first. You have already experienced the symptoms of ADHD, and your child's doctor has likely set ~~a grim picture~~ your expectations for future behavior. Understanding ADHD in more detail is good, but what you need right now is to learn the best way to parent *your* child, who also happens to have this disability called ADHD. Look for books and websites specifically about parenting a child with ADHD; all applicable titles from Dr. Edward Hallowell and Dr. Ross Greene are excellent reads on the subject. Their perspectives on raising children with ADHD and neurobehavioral disorders are very insightful and positive — they were the most helpful to my family of all the books I've read on the subject. This type of book will impart a more positive perspective and teach you how to ensure the success and happiness of your child (and their parents by extension).

> You will not find peace with ADHD until you stop asking how to fix it and start asking how to live successfully with it.

Also, look for personal experience stories that you can relate to, such as those found in the books *Easy to Love but Hard to Raise*, *The Resilient Parent*, and *Buzz: A Year of Paying Attention* (and my first book, *Boy Without Instructions*, of course). These types of books will validate your feelings and solidify that you are certainly not alone.

In all the information you consume from all the ADHD experts in magazine articles and books, there will be some suggestions that simply won't be suitable for your child. That's okay, expected even — everyone's experiences with ADHD are individual. Just move on to something else and keep learning as much as you can. The key at this point is understanding all you can about what ADHD is, how it presents, and how it can be managed most effectively during childhood.

Recognize that You Need Labels

One must define a problem first if one hopes to solve it. You can make a list of the characteristics of the problem and then address each in the hopes of finding a solution. In fact, that is the ideal way to brainstorm and achieve solutions that address the real root of a problem.

There's a general consensus that "labeling" a child is bad. That it somehow tarnishes their school record, their reputation, or maybe even their self-esteem. I do see the merit in that argument and I agree with it. In fact, I was hesitant to always refer to Ricochet's diagnoses when addressing the school at first. However, I came to the conclusion that helping my child appropriately with his particular needs would bring far more positive outcomes than the potential negative repercussions of labeling him. I was okay with a label — or six in Ricochet's case — if it acquired the help he needed.

The alphabet soup of labels — ADHD, ADD, SPD, ODD, OCD, LD, PDD, ASD, HFA, FASD, dyslexia, dysgraphia, etc. — define, at least in general terms, the challenges a child faces and what accommodations and services may be appropriate. The label is a starting point for a dialog on what that child needs in order to be academically successful. Labels from professionals are also proof ~~you're not crazy~~ of credibility to start a conversation about accommodations with the school in the first place.

> I came to the conclusion that helping my child appropriately with his particular needs would bring far more positive outcomes than the potential negative repercussions of labeling him.

Does "labeling a child" also invite assumptions of that child's weaknesses? Sure. It's inevitable. That's when it's time for my trusty fallback phrase, "So what!" I can't let a fear of how others may judge affect my course of action when it comes to raising my (misunderstood) child. I needed to accept the label, share it when necessary, and then teach Ricochet to demonstrate to the world what he *can* do and how he goes about doing it (differently). Then he will be seen for who he is once again, not what he isn't. The same goes for your child. Accept the labels — they are tools to help you advocate for your child.

Ask the Right Questions

A parent's instinct is to fix things for our kids — this is especially true for mommas. When my son was diagnosed, I researched voraciously, looking for ways to help him. What I finally discovered, two years later when we were still spinning our wheels without gaining traction, was that I was seeking answers to the wrong questions. I was chasing answers that did not exist. I was looking for ways to reduce or relieve my son's ADHD, and there just aren't any. There's no cure for ADHD — it's (one of the few things) a momma simply can't "fix."

The questions parents of children with ADHD often ask first, but *shouldn't* ask at all are:

> How do I make my child sit still?
> How do I keep my child from taking inappropriate risks?
> How do I make my child think before acting?
> How do I make my child calm instead of hyperactive?
> How do I make my child focus?
> How do I get my child to meet expectations at school?
> How do I get my child to act more maturely?

Conversely, as parents of children with ADHD, we should be asking:

> How can I help my child overcome anxiety when their schedule unexpectedly changes?

> How can I teach my child basic organizational skills?

> How can I effectively relay my child's needs to his teachers?

> What tools are available to help my child appropriately satisfy his subconscious fixation to chew everything?

> How can I teach my child that his friend not wanting to play with him today doesn't mean they are no longer friends?

> How can I teach my child to weigh consequences and rewards, to think first before acting, when that doesn't come naturally to him?

The questions we should be asking are tough questions too, but these questions have answers. Mind you, the answers are different for each child, but you can work at it until you determine the solution to each question for *your* child. Don't ask questions about eliminating symptoms (although medication and other treatments can *reduce* symptoms), but ask questions about how to keep those symptoms from hijacking your child's life, and your family.

Accept ADHD

Acceptance of anything undesirable is difficult — it goes against human nature. And this thing you didn't want, this ADHD, can wreak havoc on your child, your family, and your own life if you let it. ADHD is pervasive — it affects much of what your child does, in one way or another, in all aspects of his life.

When you seek to "fix" ADHD you have not yet reached acceptance of its role in your family. You're also setting yourself up for heavy disappointment since ADHD cannot be "fixed" — **there is no cure for ADHD.**

> You will be disappointed repeatedly as long as you continue to search for a way to "fix" it.

Fixating on repairing your child's ADHD is engaging in a vicious cycle that ~~will kill you~~ has no end. You will inevitably find a product that promises to erase ADHD (because there are many), and you'll want to erase your child's ADHD so desperately that you'll try it. You'll order this miracle merchandise and rest high on hope as you wait for your child's ADHD to be inexplicably cured — but it never will be. The product doesn't work, because you can't erase someone's ADHD.

Now you're disappointed and sad because your child still struggles with clinical-grade inattention and impulsivity. You will be disappointed repeatedly as long as you continue to search for a way to "fix" it. Many seasoned parents in the ADHD community call this the search for the magic bullet. I can save you lots of time trolling the Internet for a magic bullet by telling you right now: there is no magic bullet. Believe me, I know. I was a desperate, new-to-ADHD parent once, too. I spent a couple of years searching for a magic bullet myself. I spent those years getting jacked up on hope and then crashing into despair when the latest product, gadget, diet, supplement, therapy, or treatment that promised extraordinary change didn't improve my son's ADHD.

After a couple of years, I recognized the pattern and realized for myself that there's no magic bullet for Ricochet. I then learned to ask the right questions, and I accepted my child's ADHD. Those right questions meant I spent my time productively, looking for effective ways to help my child live with ADHD instead of circling the drain in that dark vortex of I-need-to-fix-it-but-can't-figure-out-how despair.

Accept ADHD as soon as possible. Do it for yourself, and for the benefit of your child. Our children are smart and observant little people. If they see you constantly looking for ways to "fix" them, they will internalize that there must be something wrong with them, leading to shame, embarrassment, and low self-esteem. To the contrary, if you accept their ADHD, help them implement strategies and tools to cope with it, and focus on their *abilities*, you will build their self-confidence instead of further tearing it down.

Go ahead and recognize and accept that your child has a *disability* as well now. A disability is defined as "a disqualification, restriction, or disadvantage." ADHD definitely meets that definition! I wish someone would have placed this definition in front of me when Ricochet was diagnosed with ADHD — maybe I wouldn't have walked around with blinders on for the first two and a half years, insisting that ADHD was only a "difference." Anyone who has ADHD has a disability. Accepting this allows you to stop looking for a "fix" and focus on raising a happy, healthy, successful child in spite of his disability.

> *If you accept their ADHD, help them implement strategies and tools to cope with it, and focus on their abilities, you will build their self-confidence instead of further tearing it down.*

Employ New Tools

Parents are regularly provided information on developmental milestones from birth through early childhood and beyond. Some parents compare their children to these typical milestones and worry about them often, especially if they are first-time parents. Repeat parents will compare each new child's development to their experiences with their older children when they were that particular age.

Once we have evaluated the developmental milestones our pediatrician defined as "normal," we compare our children to their peers at the playground or in the classroom. We are constantly measuring our children's growth and development against what we are told is "normal" to make sure they are growing and developing as expected. This system of evaluation works for most parents, but "normal" milestones are not a fair assessment for children like ours.

Parents of children with ADHD must recognize and accept that a child with ADHD is developmentally younger than the number of years since they were born. When dealing with a developmental disorder like ADHD, parents have to develop a new frame of reference. For instance, my twelve-year-old son is old enough by traditional standards to handle disappointment without ~~exploding~~ tears and/or an outburst. However, the characteristics of ADHD need to be the deciding factor in his ability to effectively handle disappointment — the nuances of ADHD say he can be twelve and not handle disappointment like an twelve-year-old should. By using ADHD as my new frame of reference, I can identify that this reaction to disappointment could very well be typical for my child.

Calendar age is not a suitable tool to measure the behavior of a child with ADHD.

It's so important to your child's self-esteem, not to mention your sanity, to use the appropriate yardstick to measure your child's behavior. This new and different gauge is appropriately developed by taking into account his ADHD, any other disabilities or disorders such as learning disabilities or anxiety, and his actual level of maturity. Calendar age is not a suitable tool to measure the behavior of a child with ADHD.

Your child's self-esteem will take another blow it doesn't need every time you instill expectations that are unattainable to your child. Now, I'm not suggesting that you use ADHD as an excuse for inappropriate behavior (more on that in *Step 5: Make a Plan, Find the Discipline Balance*) — I'm saying you must scale your expectations to your child's *actual* abilities. You should still expect appropriate behavior and teach your child the lagging skills they need to meet those expectations eventually.

Self-esteem is boosted through accomplishment, so your child needs to be reminded, through experiencing actual successful outcomes, that they can meet your expectations and achieve other goals set for them. If they don't have frequent opportunities to feel successful at something, they will trudge through life feeling like a failure and give up on trying altogether at some point. While academic achievement isn't ~~life or death~~ the be-all and end-all that many make it out to be, frequent achievement in one area or another is crucial to healthy self-esteem.

Employing a different, more appropriate yardstick to measure your child's actions is beneficial to parents of kids with ADHD as well. Giving your child the same commands day after day without projected results is frustrating and defeating — it just doesn't feel good. You're hurting yourself as well as your child when your expectations aren't tailored to your child's special needs because then your expectations simply aren't realistic. Set attainable goals and use new tools to measure progress for your child.

Focus on the Positive

Now that you've accepted that ADHD is going to be part of your life and part of your child's life, you can focus on the positive. This is *most* crucial. Positivity and negativity are both multipliers and magnets for their likenesses. When you are pessimistic, negativity takes over and you attract more negativity. When you are optimistic, you feel good all-around and you attract more positivity.

Be mindful of your tone of voice, facial expressions, and body language around your child as well. The desperation on your face may be genuine, but it's also detrimental to your child. I try to live only in a place of truth, but that particular truth — the sadness and desperation that sometimes accompanies this special parenthood — further tears down your child. Your job is to build them up. Provide a solid foundation and build them up through a positive attitude and focus.

I know it's hard to be positive when your child is first diagnosed with ADHD or even when things aren't going great with ADHD behaviors long after. I get that because I've been there. Sometimes I still live there. But I also know it's possible to be optimistic in spite of ADHD. I'll take it a step further — it's even possible to be positive in light of ADHD, as ADHD's mirror traits are often beneficial in the workforce and life in general.

* The following table of *Mirror Traits* was copied from world-renowned ADHD expert, Dr. Edward Hallowell's website, DrHallowell.com. [1]

Negative Trait Associated with ADHD	to	Accompanying Positive Mirror Trait
Hyperactive, restless	is	Energetic
Intrusive	is	Eager
Can't stay on point	is	Sees connections others don't
Forgetful	is	Gets totally into what he is doing
Disorganized	is	Spontaneous
Stubborn	is	Persistent, won't give up
Inconsistent	is	Shows flashes of brilliance
Moody	is	Sensitive

Once I accepted that I couldn't fix my son's ADHD, it freed a lot of space in my heart and mind to consider and nurture his talents and successes.

Will he win the school spelling bee? Probably not, but it's certainly possible he could achieve third place, and third place in a spelling bee is definitely an accomplishment worth celebrating.

Will he have the neatest book project? Nope. That will never happen due to dysgraphia. We can praise him for finishing the project with a good attitude and turning it in on time though. That may not be much of an accomplishment for a neurotypical kid, but it's a huge achievement for my kid.

A vital part of parenting a special needs child is adjusting your frame of reference in determining what is worthy of praise. While your parents may have only celebrated your trophies and tangible awards growing up, you must adjust your expectations and create a new definition of success tailored to your child. This one adjustment alone will have a sustained and positive effect on you and your child's outlook.

We will delve into discovering your child's gifts and talents in more detail in *Step 4: Get to Know Your Child*. For now, make a conscious effort to ask the right questions in your search for ways to cope with ADHD and adjust your frame of reference so you can focus on the positive.

ADHD FACT SHEET

The following facts about ADHD have been compiled from different sources, including experts in the field and my own experiences. As you read through these facts, highlight the top three to five that set off a light-bulb moment for you — they could be facts you didn't know, facts that clear up misconceptions, or things you just want to focus on improving with your child. Feel free to post this list as a family reminder, too.

A CHILD WITH ADHD...

» has trouble paying attention due to a neurological difference.
» may exhibit impulsive behaviors.
» usually longs to meet expectations and please parents and elders.
» is sometimes overly active.
» can be more prone to injury.
» cannot pass ADHD on to others; it is not contagious.
» has a probability of also having sensory processing disorder, a learning disability, behavioral disorder, or other mental health condition.
» will have a hard time resisting temptation.
» needs treatment to prevent ADHD from controlling their life.
» is unable to organize, and may also struggle with sequencing and planning.
» doesn't seem to listen when spoken to, but often does.
» avoids dislikes.
» can focus on something for hours, if it is something that interests them or if they get a great deal of sensory stimulation from it.
» may interrupt or blurt out answers.
» can be very smart.
» is often less mature than their peers.
» probably has trouble with working memory.
» may be prone to losing things.
» probably has a low frustration tolerance.
» can show emotional reactivity, including changing moods quickly and taking things personally.
» will quite possibly be able to do the same task successfully tomorrow that they couldn't do today.
» may seem restless a majority of the time.
» will miss steps or not remember what to do after step one when given multi-step directions.
» wants rules and clearly defined expectations to help with self-regulation.
» may struggle socially and need help deciphering social cues.
» needs you to advocate for them.
» **is as worthy of love and respect as any other child.**

RESEARCH RECORD

You are going to be reading a lot of books and articles on ADHD as you learn to parent your child. Use this table to record each item you read for future reference.

DATE	TITLE & AUTHOR
/ /	
	AH-HA's
	What did you learn?

DATE	TITLE & AUTHOR
/ /	
	AH-HA's

DATE	TITLE & AUTHOR
/ /	
	AH-HA's

ASK THE **RIGHT** QUESTIONS

Learning to ask the <u>right questions</u> is essential for your mental health as a parent of a child with ADHD. The wrong questions are those that seek to "fix" ADHD or eliminate its symptoms. The <u>right questions</u> are those that search for ADHD management strategies and skill improvement. List questions specific to your child and their ADHD below.

What questions do you have about your child's behavior

WHO
WHAT
WHERE
WHEN
WHY
HOW

» _____

» _____

» _____

» _____

» _____

» _____

» _____

» _____

» _____

After completing your list of questions, use this litmus test to see if each question fits into the "right" questions requirement.
1. Am I trying to eliminate one of my child's ADHD symptoms?
2. Is my question looking for an "easy answer" or a "cure"?
Strike through that question if you answer "yes" to #1 or #2 above — that means it's a question that has no answer. Better yet, consider if it can be reworded to qualify as a "right question" first — if not, strike it off your list.

YOUR NEW COMPASS

Positive and realistic goals for a child with ADHD

North points to positive and realistic goals for a child with ADHD. Fill in the south with the "wrong questions." Park inappropriate expectations in the parking lot at the bottom when they come to mind.

Parking Lot for Inappropriate Expectations

Wrong Questions

FOCUS ON THE POSITIVE

Record the wonderful qualities of your child. Don't skip this because you think you already know what's great about your child. It's important to go through the act of writing it down. Ask your child what they think are their positive attributes and record them on this page as well. (That helps to direct their compass to the positive, too.)

Positive Traits

Interests

Talents

Step 2: Assemble Your Team

»»»»»»»»

"Let our advance worrying become advance thinking and planning."

—Winston Churchill

If it takes a village to raise a child, it must require ~~China's entire population~~ an army to successfully raise a child with ADHD. Seriously. An entire army.

There are a lot more people involved in the well-being of our children than just their parents and close family, ADHD or not. There are doctors, school teachers, coaches, art/dance/karate instructors, etc. who all have an influence in shaping who our children become.

For example, I didn't become an athletic individual because my Little League softball coach threw a bat at me, after a swing and miss, when I was seven or eight years old. I thought all coaches were hot-heads like him, so I avoided athletics for that reason. I did, however, develop a love of science from a positive experience with a high school biology teacher who was quirky and funny and real (that's your shout-out, Mr. Otero).

Everyone in our children's lives is an influence on who they become in one way or another. That's especially true for children with ADHD, autism, or other neuro-behavioral disorders because their self-image is exceptionally fragile.

No one treatment works for every child. In fact, the American Academy of Pediatrics advises, as studies have proven, that a combination of treatments is the most effective in treating ADHD[2]. Each part of treatment is administered by a different specialist, so you will assemble a team to ensure the most effective care for your child with ADHD.

Start with the village that influences all children: doctors, school teachers, coaches, art/dance/karate instructors, etc. Make sure they know and understand as much of your child's special needs as is relevant to their relationship with your child. Then add in the members specific to your child's special needs: occupational therapists, counselors/psychotherapists, school guidance counselors, school psychologists, school special education personnel, school at-risk and 504 committee members, school administration, medical ADHD specialists (in addition to the pediatrician), an ADHD coach, nutritionists maybe, etc., etc. Don't forget extended family and friends, too. Knowledge, compassion, and understanding from all of these individuals are required to fulfill and nurture our children.

> Everyone in our children's lives is an influence on who they become in one way or another. That's especially true for children with ADHD, autism, or other neuro-behavioral disorders because their self-image is exceptionally fragile.

That's an army, and they will all have a substantial influence on the individual your child will become. These individuals have the potential to mean the difference between a life overwhelmed and diminished by ADHD, or a life full of joy and success despite ADHD. I know which fate I choose for my child, and I'm certain I know your choice as well.

Let's look at each potential member of your team in more detail…

ADHD Treatment Doctor

Neurologist, Behavioral Specialist, Behavioral Pediatrician, Psychopharmacologist, or Psychiatrist

This is the individual who will track your child's medical progress as it relates to ADHD. They may have diagnosed the ADHD as well. If you choose to utilize medication as part of your child's ADHD treatment plan, this is the professional who will prescribe those medications and track side effects and efficacy.

Behavioral Therapy

Counselor, Psychotherapist, Psychologist, Clinical Social Worker or Applied Behavioral Specialist (ABA)

Most people have a negative opinion of psychotherapy, feeling there must be something "wrong" with you if you need to see a "shrink." Our society harshly judges those who seek the counsel of a therapist. Shame from your friends and family or not, your child with ADHD will benefit greatly from counseling, and so will your entire family. This professional will guide you through the day-to-day of parenting a child with ADHD and also teach you how to implement long-term strategies for your child and your family.

Having been with and without therapy, I can tell you with certainty that life with a child with ADHD is greatly improved with expert guidance and someone neutral to bounce problems off.

Ricochet and I see a Licensed Clinical Social Worker and Play Therapist twice a month for ADHD guidance. She helps me with systems and strategies for everyday parenting of a child who has ADHD. She also spends time one-on-one with Ricochet, working on skills such as frustration tolerance and social skills through play therapy. Warrior Girl sees her once a month for sibling-of-ADHD issues and her own anxiety as well.

We did not have counseling the first year of Ricochet's diagnosis due to lousy health insurance. Having been with and without it, I can tell you with certainty that life with a child with ADHD is greatly improved with expert guidance and someone neutral to bounce problems off. Be sure to select a therapist who specializes in pediatric and adolescent ADHD.

Occupational Therapy (OT)

Occupational therapy is a service most parents don't know to consider for treatment of ADHD. A pediatric OT offers therapy for sensory processing, auditory processing, muscle development, bodily awareness, and even impulse control. According to Lucy Jane Miller, PhD, director of the Sensory Processing Treatment and Research (STAR) Center at the Children's Hospital in Denver, 40 percent of children with ADHD or sensory processing disorder have symptoms of both (and I've heard speculation it may be as much as 95 percent). Also, up to 50 percent of children with auditory processing disorder have ADHD.[3]

We began OT to improve Ricochet's handwriting and motor coordination when he was six years old. The occupational therapists immediately detected sensory issues and worked on that with him as well. After a year of visits, his handwriting hadn't improved much, but I had gained perspective on what causes many of Ricochet's actions and reactions. We accumulated valuable information and behavioral strategies through OT that explained so much of why Ricochet has particular behaviors and taught me skills to help him feel more comfortable in certain situations. Besides all of that understanding and knowledge gained, he had a great time running, bouncing, and crashing much more wildly than allowed at home, and he enjoyed playing with other kids who have similar differences.

I strongly recommend that you add OT to your child's treatment if at all possible. It can be done intermittently on an as-needed basis or long-term. Having an occupational therapist is almost as important to me in Ricochet's treatment as having behavioral therapy.

Speech Therapy (SLT)

Children with ADHD can often benefit from speech therapy, even if they don't have a specific disability that affects their speech. A speech therapist can also work with a child on better communication in social situations, study skills like organization and planning, and classroom accommodations based on the individual communication needs of the child. If you see a communication breakdown with your child with ADHD, contact a speech therapist for an evaluation.

School Team

You need a lot of school personnel on your side if your child with ADHD attends school outside the home. A lot of time and effort is required to coordinate all these people and the special educational needs of your child, but it's vitally important. Please don't hide your child's ADHD diagnosis from school

Homeschool

If you homeschool, there are likely still individuals outside your home who will work with your child in an educational capacity. Maybe you participate in homeschool activities at the local children's science museum or art gallery. The instructors of these groups need to be educated about the needs of your child as well.

personnel! That will cause a lot of undue stress and heartache when he is expected to conduct himself like his neurotypical peers but can't.

Instead, make many teachers and administrators at your child's school aware of his special needs. This should include everyone that comes in contact with your child during his school week and everyone who has influence over implementing accommodations for him in the educational environment to ensure academic success — don't forget the gym coach and the music teacher as they are vital to your child's success as well.

We will dive much deeper into the subject of school rights and accommodations for kids with ADHD in *Step 7: Get a Handle on ADHD at School*.

ADHD Coach

I do not have personal experience with ADHD coaching, but I know it's a valuable tool for teens and adults with ADHD, and it's a tool I plan to use when my son is older, if it's accessible to us.

According to the Edge Foundation — an organization whose mission is to ensure students with ADHD get coaching services to finish their education and realize their full potential — an ADHD coach helps people meet the unique challenges of ADHD and opportunities life presents[4].

People have been using coaches outside of athletics for decades now. Executives may use a coach to help them achieve professional excellence. A life coach may be hired to help someone reach a life-long goal. There are coaches for becoming an author and losing weight, too. All of these coaches help people overcome hurdles and meet their life goals just as a sports coach helps their athletes improve their game and meet their athletic goals. They all approach coaching in much the same way, too — by targeting your hurdles, teaching you the skills to improve and surpass the hurdles, and holding you accountable until you reach your goal.

Life coaches look for weaknesses that can diminish your productivity and keep you from reaching your potential and goals, such as poor time management and a lack of organization skills. They then help you develop these skills and check in with you regularly to see if you are meeting the benchmarks you created together. ADHD coaching is essentially the same except that ADHD coaches specialize in the challenges of ADHD, too. They target the skills an individual with ADHD needs to further develop, and they work with the individual one-on-one to improve. You may not have lofty aspirations, but you are working toward a goal whenever you are trying to improve something.

Goals for a student with ADHD might include:

› being late to class only one time a month,

› consistently bringing home all materials to complete homework assignments,

› turning in all homework assignments,

› asking for help when needed,

› successfully planning and executing long-term projects,

› etc.

You may be worried that you can't find an ADHD coach where you live, but you shouldn't be concerned with geography when it comes to coaching. Most coaches are structured to work with clients over the phone and/or through Skype. To find a reputable coach for your child, reach out to the IAAC (adhdcoachinstitute.org), the International Coach Federation (coachfederation.org), the ADHD Coaches Organization (ACO; adhdcoaches.org), or the Edge Foundation (edgefoundation.org).

Nutrition

Diet and nutrition can play a role, both positive and negative, in how your child's ADHD presents. Additives like artificial food dyes, artificial flavors, nitrites, and other chemicals added to processed foods in the United States can exacerbate ADHD symptoms such as hyperactivity and mood. It is often suggested that these additives and many other edible items be removed from the diet of individuals with ADHD, who are often more sensitive to chemical additives.

Special programs like the Feingold Diet, a Gluten-Free Diet (GF), a Casein-Free Diet (CF), or a Gluten-Free & Casein-Free Diet (GFCF) are used by some as part of their ADHD treatment with success. Yet, there are many others who have tried these diets with no discernible improvement in ADHD symptoms. It is my feeling that individuals who see marked improvement in ADHD symptoms by implementing special diets had a food allergy or sensitivity that was presenting as ADHD or exacerbating ADHD symptoms — the change in diet didn't directly treat ADHD.

There are also foods and supplements recommended to be added to the diets of those with ADHD, such as Omega 3/Fish Oil, magnesium, and foods high in protein.

The science is slim on the real efficacy of diet and nutrition as a stand-alone treatment for ADHD, and ADHD expert opinions vary widely on the subject as well. I will not get into more detail about the role of nutrition in ADHD treatment in this book since there isn't any broad consensus in the scientific community about the efficacy of diet changes in treating ADHD. There are some great books on the role of diet and nutrition as it relates to ADHD, however. If this interests you, consider reading *Healing the New Childhood*

Epidemics by Kenneth Bock, or *Healing ADD* by Dr. Daniel Amen. You can also visit a nutritionist or dietician regularly for guidance.

I will share my experiences with nutrition and supplementation regarding Ricochet. We tried a strictly gluten-free diet for Ricochet for over a year with no noticeable difference where his ADHD is concerned. We also eliminated dairy at one point and saw no ADHD symptom improvement with that either. We limit Ricochet's intake of processed foods full of artificial colors, flavors, and chemicals as much as possible, and that does make a bit of difference.

Ricochet has also tried many supplements over the years with zero or negative results. He has been taking over-the-counter fish oil for at least three years now, and I haven't seen any change I can attribute to it. He has tried magnesium, calcium, and B vitamins all with nasty mood-related side effects. My kid is such a puzzle!

Just this year we had a Neurogenomic Profile blood test done through our Integrative Medicine physician. That revealed that Ricochet has genetic abnormalities in the DNA responsible for detoxification (he'd had a prior test that showed heavy metal toxicity for no discernable reason), neurotransmitter production, and other cell processes that affect mood and behavior. We have been giving him special supplements to help with these broken biological processes, but it's too soon to tell if they will fuel some improvement.

All of the nutritional and alternative methods we have tried have yet to show ADHD symptom reduction in my child, but that doesn't mean they won't be helpful for your child. Through all these trials, I accepted that medication is a part of Ricochet's life, at least while he is young, and that's okay. We combine some nutritional improvements, supplements, and medication for a tailored treatment that (mostly) works for him.

Investigating the efficacy of nutritional changes is certainly worth a try for everyone with ADHD, but usually isn't enough treatment alone.

Neurofeedback and "Brain Games"

There are many treatments available that work to retrain neural pathways in the brain. These treatments are thought to reduce ADHD symptoms in some people. To take advantage of this methodology, talk to your child's therapist. Psychiatrists with specific training can perform neurofeedback in their offices. You can expect to visit at least three times a week for effective results. There are also at-home neurofeedback-type programs available.

Some think it's beneficial in much the same manner to play "brain games." These can usually be found online, such as luminosity.com, but you can also find "brain games" that function on handheld electronic devices like a Nintendo DS or a tablet app.

Ricochet has not participated in any of these programs, so I cannot offer personal experience about them. It is important to note that there aren't many scientific studies that prove or debunk the efficacy of neurofeedback and "brain games" as treatment for ADHD.

Your Peeps

Having a behaviorally-challenged child can be very isolating. I didn't see myself in other mommas. I didn't see my child in other children. I felt like the only parent of a child who couldn't behave. I avoided the school water cooler, birthday parties, and playdates. Eventually, I found myself detached from the people around me because I could no longer relate.

Find your ~~sanity~~ people — you know, the ones who understand what it's like to parent a child with ADHD. Whether it is on the Internet or in person, be sure to find parents with a similar parenting experience and converse with each other often. Having this sense of community is therapeutic and necessary for your own self-care.

There are many blogs on ADHD, and many have a thriving community. You can find forums, listservs, and Facebook pages on ADHD, too. The Internet is a great place to start to instantly be part of an active community who understands your parenting challenges and can offer support.

Having this type of in-person relationship is helpful as well. Look for ADHD support groups locally (usually through CHADD, a non-profit, or your local hospital), or invite another parent who has a child with ADHD to meet for coffee. I meet two mommas who also have kids with ADHD one or two times a month for coffee. We vent, we ask for opinions, we laugh, we cry. What you do when you get together informally for support isn't really important, it's just knowing you have people in your corner who understand you that makes a difference.

These people who understand what you are going through are just as important on your team as treatment and therapy. Get together with your people on a regular basis to prevent isolation. The acceptance will be such a relief.

Frequently Evaluate Your Team

If at first you don't succeed… try, try again. If one of your team members isn't working out, go to a new provider. If one of these treatment options is ineffective for your child, discontinue it and try something else. That's the nature of this ADHD treatment game. **Every child with ADHD is truly individual.** Some respond better than others to behavioral therapy or diet changes. Each stimulant medication will affect each child uniquely as well. ADHD medication success often requires trying different medications and different dosages — it's not like taking Tylenol for a headache.

In the interest of keeping it real, I must disclose that your treatment plan will be a moving target. Knowing that at the beginning will make your journey learning to parent your child with ADHD a little easier. Be sure to keep a daily journal corresponding to all current treatments for your child so you can determine the efficacy of each treatment and adjust your treatment plan accordingly. Your journal should include: medications and supplements with dosages and time taken; food intake with times, description of activity levels and moods several times a day with their corresponding times; activities throughout the day, especially those out of the norm; and sleep and wake times. A journal worksheet is included in *Step 4: Get to Know Your Child*. You have to record every detail of their day to get a clear picture of the efficacy of their treatment and potential behavioral triggers. Managing your child's ADHD is work, like getting an additional job ~~almost~~.

Our special brand of parenthood is a challenge, that's for sure. Don't try to go it alone — assemble a team to ensure the best possible care for your child with ADHD, and for you.

ASSEMBLE YOUR TEAM

Your team is enormously important when parenting a child with ADHD. There are many players, all with different roles in your child's treatment. Use this page to log your service providers.

NAME | PHONE | NOTES

Treatment Doctor	Behavioral Therapy
Occupational Therapy	ADHD Coach

Nutritionist or Dietician	Alternative Therapy Providers
Other	Other

NAME | PHONE | NOTES

ASSEMBLE YOUR TEAM

Your team is enormously important when parenting a child with ADHD. There are many players, all with different roles in your child's treatment. Use this page to log your educational team members.

NAME | PHONE | NOTES | EMAIL

Teacher	Resource Teacher (if applicable)
Guidance Counselor	School Psychologist

School Occupational Therapist	Principal/Headmaster
Director of Special Services/Exceptional Children	Other

NAME | PHONE | NOTES | EMAIL

YOUR PEEPS

It's important to communicate with other parents who understand your special brand of parenting. Make a plan to start interacting with other parents of kids with neuro-behavioral disorders.

What	Contact
Websites & Forums	
{a mom's view of ADHD}	http://amomsviewofadhd.com
Easy to Love but Hard to Raise	http://easytolovebut.com
ADDconnect (Community + Forum for ADDitude Magazine)	http://addconnect.com http://additudemag.com
ADDmoms	http://ADDmoms.com
ADD Forums, Parenting Section	http://www.addforums.com
Daily Strength	http://www.dailystrength.org/c/Parents-of-Children-With-ADHD/support-group
LD Online	http://www.ldonline.org/

What	Contact
ADHD Active Conversations on Facebook	
Keeping it Real about Parenting ADHD	PennyWilliamsAuthor
{a mom's view of ADHD}	a-moms-view-of-ADHD
Easy to Love but Hard to Raise	easytolovekids
ADHD Aware	ADHDAware
ADHD Hope	ADHDhope
Support for Parents of Children with ADD/ADHD	ADD.ADHDSupport
Parents of Children with ADHD Group	https://www.facebook.com/groups/2373657488/?ref=br_rs
Moms Helping Moms with ADHD Kids Group	https://www.facebook.com/groups/47204695379/

YOUR PEEPS

Local Support Groups (Search online for a support group in your area.)	

People You Know (Think about other parents you know who have kids with similar special needs or even friends of friends. Invite them to meet for coffee or something informal.)	

A Word About Medication

The traditional ADHD treatment includes stimulant medications such as Ritalin, Concerta, Daytrana, Adderall, Vyvanse, etc. Sometimes non-stimulants, like Straterra, are prescribed for ADHD, but much less often. Eighty percent of individuals with ADHD will experience reduced symptoms with a stimulant medication. The other 20 percent will find stimulants ineffective[5]. And of the 80 percent who find medication beneficial to treat their ADHD, each individual's reaction to each medication can be different. My son cannot take Adderall or Vyvanse, because they both make him volatile and dangerous, but I know many children who have great success with these medications. What works for Peter may not work for Paul, and vice versa, when it comes to pharmaceuticals and ADHD. That's ADHD medication in a nutshell.

I will not go into detail about medication in this book. First, giving your child ADHD medication is a very personal decision, and not everyone will chose that treatment path. Secondly, the subject of ADHD medication is very complex, and advice on it should be limited to medical professionals, that which I am not.

However, I have a great deal of experience with using ADHD medications to treat my child's ADHD as well as a dash of been-there-done-that wisdom I want to share with those who are considering or have already chosen medication as part of their child's ADHD treatment. Even if you are opposed to medication right now, I encourage you to read what I have to say about it. This information may prove useful to you at some point in the future.

A WORD ABOUT MEDICATION

Finding effective medication for Ricochet has been the toughest part of my parenting journey with him so far. Yet, I am ironically passionate about using this tool as part of a child's ADHD treatment.

The medication discussion is inserted in this point in the guide because effective treatment of the core ADHD symptoms is essential to successfully parenting a child with ADHD. If your child can't slow down enough to learn skills, routines, and systems they need in order to manage their ADHD, they won't be able to reach their potential level of improvement. I'm not saying you have to use traditional pharmaceuticals like stimulants or even non-stimulants — I recognize that this is a decision that must be made on an individual level — but it is crucial that you find some form of treatment that can manage your child's symptoms enough that they can learn new skills and practice self-regulation. There's a candid saying in the ADHD community: "Pills don't teach skills." That summarizes the approach you must take to ADHD treatment — medication will not "fix" everything, but it will allow your child to learn the skills they lack but need to have to cope and live successfully with ADHD. Medication (i.e., "pills") isn't enough on its own to manage ADHD effectively; you also have to teach the lagging skills — this is crucial to remember.

Mr. T and I chose medication for our son for two reasons: (1) behavioral modification had been implemented for a long time prior to diagnosis with no real success, and (2) Ricochet was very sad and defeated the majority of days, at *just five years old*. He often told me, "I am stupid, and I can't do anything right," despite having an IQ in the 130s (that's like the 95th percentile of intelligence), and despite really wanting to please. Ricochet was like Tigger — a well-known character in *Winnie the Pooh* — before ADHD treatment, he was bouncing around exuberantly and creating destruction, hurting his relationships, and always feeling remorseful after.

For us, the decision to give Ricochet medication for his ADHD was made simply to improve his quality of life. To save his life, truthfully, if I'm honest with myself about how sad and defeated he really was back then. He couldn't slow down enough to begin to learn the skills necessary to cope with ADHD, much less self-regulate, and his behavior was so wild he was constantly in trouble. We saw the enormous potential in this kind-hearted, smart boy, and we were watching it get trampled and diminished amid the chaos of ADHD. If medication was going to help our son achieve success and happiness, we'd be foolish not to try it.

And so we did. *Oh my Lord, the medication trials!* I want to curl up in the fetal position just thinking about it. Thank goodness what doesn't kill us makes us stronger — I'm one strong momma now!

Over the last five years, Ricochet tried every stimulant medication on the market plus Strattera and many medications used off-label for ADHD. The first three years were a constant struggle to find a medication that didn't lose effectiveness after just two months, like clockwork. It was a roller-coaster ride of peaks of hope and severe drops into valleys of despair.

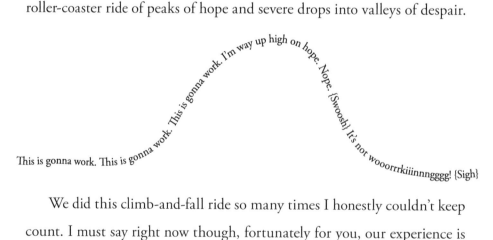

This is gonna work. This is gonna work. This is gonna work. I'm way up high on hope. Nope. {Swoosh} It's not wooorrrkiiinnngggg! {Sigh}

We did this climb-and-fall ride so many times I honestly couldn't keep count. I must say right now though, fortunately for you, our experience is *not* typical. I believe the average individual with ADHD may try one or two medications and a few different dosages to find something that works to reduce their ADHD symptoms. Ricochet is a different case because stimulants keep losing effectiveness every two months, or he has a serious side effect that warrants immediate discontinuation.

After trying every stimulant on its own, he went back to the one that was the most effective with the least side effects and began adding other medications to supplement it. His doctor was hoping a combination of medications would sustain efficacy. This stimulant was like a magic pill for Ricochet at first, when it was working; he was calm and attentive, and medication even improved his dysgraphia (handwriting disability). But then it failed so quickly each time we increased the dose and never worked as well as it did the first few weeks he was taking it. His doctor and I added a few different anti-depressants and anxiety medications one at a time with freakish results; Ricochet was so sensitive to these types of medications that he had some of the super-rare and intolerable side effects, like hallucinations, extreme fear, and suicidality. After three failed attempts, I knew those types of medications were not going to work for my boy.

Ricochet sees a Behavioral Pediatrician who has been practicing medicine in this specialty for at least three decades, I believe. He has seen and treated a lot of kids with ADHD in that time. This is a real benefit to our family because he had Ricochet try an old influenza medication that is now sometimes prescribed for Parkinson's and off-label for ADHD. I've only met one other person whose child with ADHD was prescribed this medicine among the hundreds and hundreds I've chatted with online — it's that rare to be prescribed for ADHD. He added this medication to the stimulant that was found to be the best in the bunch for Ricochet, and the stimulant held its efficacy for well over a year.

Halleluiah! We were off the medication roller coaster, at least for a while.

For over a year, this medication combination worked for Ricochet until the two medications together seemed to cause some extreme fear episodes. His doctor changed the stimulant he was taking to a new stimulant on the market he hadn't tried yet and kept the added supplemental medicine. That was a good change, and all was well again, for a while.

When I say "all was well," I must quantify it by pointing out that I'm speaking relatively. Are his medications magic pills that erase his ADHD when he takes them? No. Not even close. His medication greatly reduces his ADHD symptoms, enough that he can learn skills and routines through behavior modification and therapy, and enough to sort of get by in school. Really, it is enough to get by in school in terms of ADHD alone — his biggest struggles in that environment right now are his learning disabilities and non-existent social skills.

We recently had to discontinue the old influenza medication because the fear episodes returned with a vengeance. We are again on the seek-try-hope-try again roller coaster of ADHD medication trials. You are probably wondering why in the world this crazy woman I keep trying. The truth is, even failing medications are better than no medication for Ricochet. Without any pharmaceutical intervention, he can't slow down enough to focus on one thing for more than three to five minutes, and cannot focus enough to learn the compensatory skills and strategies he needs to achieve success. Medication is a requirement for Ricochet, and I've accepted that.

Giving your child medication for ADHD is tough, in many ways. It is hard for just about every momma to accept giving your child a "controlled substance" every day. Sometimes, it's tough simply to get them to take it. And the trial and error to find an effective medication is exhausting, especially if you're at it for longer than normal, as I have been. But all of that is well worth it in the end, when your child is achieving some success and happiness. If I can say that after all we've been through with medication, then there's a good chance it will be true for you as well.

Following, are my tips on ADHD medication for those readers who will implement a medication regimen as part of their child's ADHD treatment:

› Accept that the first medication and the first dosage prescribed are not likely to be right for your child. They are a starting point from which dosage can be adjusted until effective.

› Realize that, when starting stimulant medication, your child's behavior (and even personality) may get worse for a few days before it gets better. Try to stick with a particular medication for at least a week, unless your child has severe side effects. If you feel something is wrong with a particular medication early on, call your prescribing doctor and relay your experiences right away. If your intuition tells you something is wrong, call the doctor no matter how long your child has been on that particular medication. Your prescribing doctor is the ultimate resource when it comes to your child's medications — don't rely on forum stalkers for information about what your child is experiencing with their medication. If you have doubts, discuss them with the doctor.

› Know that medication is not going to "erase" your child's ADHD symptoms, not even during the hours the medication is effective each day. When medication is effective for ADHD, it calms the brain and allows more focus, more thinking things through, and a calmer activity level. "More" is the operative word — medication does not "cure" ADHD.

› Remember that a medication that works great for time spent at home may not be effective enough for the extra demands on the specific skills that are often lagging in kids with ADHD but required by school.

› Know that you can always stop a medication if the side effects outweigh the benefits. Consult your prescribing physician on the best way to stop that particular medication first — some medications prescribed for ADHD have to be tapered off slowly.

A WORD ABOUT MEDICATION

> Don't let anyone tell you medication can't work for your child until you've tried every type of medication possible for ADHD. When Ricochet's great stimulant failed again after the second dosage increase, his doctor at the time (no longer our doctor for Ricochet's ADHD) said, "You might just have to accept that this is as good as it gets for him with medicine." I had seen better already, and I wasn't going to accept that so early in the game. Good thing I didn't because we eventually found effective medication for him for a couple years, under the guidance of a different doctor.

> If your child loses their personality or is a "zombie" on medication, their current medication or dosage is *not* right for them. Stimulant medication is not intended to dope a child into submission, and this effect usually means the dosage is way too high. Your child's personality will shine through if the medication and dosage are accurate. Don't settle for anything less.

> Trust your gut! You know your child best. If side effects are severe but your doctor is telling you to give the medication a month, you may need to put your foot down. If your child is not themselves on the medication, demand a change. A parent's intuition is a powerful compass.

A great chart of all medications for ADHD, sorted by type, is available by visiting http://www.myadhd.com/treatment_tools/medicationchart.html.

WEIGH THE RISKS

You may be concerned about the potential risks and side effects of ADHD stimulant medication. It's important to consider the risks of not giving your child medication as well. There are certainly risks to that, too. Finish the lists with your own fears and insights, then weigh the two columns. This activity is likely to be an ah-ha for you.

RISKS OF MEDICATION

- Loss of appetite
- Trouble sleeping
- Stunting growth
- Death in patients with undiagnosed pre-existing heart conditions
- Change their brain
- _____
- _____
- _____
- _____
- _____
- _____
- _____
- _____
- _____

NOW PRIORITIZE THEM TO ESTABLISH THE ORDER YOU'LL TACKLE THEM IN:

- More impulsive, so more prone to injury
- More likely to abuse drugs and alcohol
- Poor academic performance
- Poor self-esteem
- Few or no friends
- In trouble all the time
- At greater risk of traffic accidents
- _____
- _____
- _____
- _____
- _____
- _____

MEDICATION TRACKER

Use this chart to log your child's ADHD medication daily. This is invaluable information to share with the prescribing doctor if you are having medication issues.

DATE / /

MEDICATION NAME, TIME, DOSE

POSITIVE OUTCOMES WITH TIMES

NEGATIVE OUTCOMES WITH TIMES

BE DETAILED!

DATE / /

MEDICATION NAME, TIME, DOSE

POSITIVE OUTCOMES WITH TIMES

NEGATIVE OUTCOMES WITH TIMES

DATE / /

MEDICATION NAME, TIME, DOSE

POSITIVE OUTCOMES WITH TIMES

NEGATIVE OUTCOMES WITH TIMES

Step 3: Create Structure

>>>>>>>>>>

"In fiction: we find the predictable boring. In real life: we find the unpredictable terrifying."

—Mokokoma Mokhonoana

Children with ADHD do not have the intrinsic planning and organization skills that most individuals do. Therefore, they are less able to create their own structure than their neurotypical peers. Creating structure in the world around them, external structure, helps to fill this gap. A routine and predictable schedule pre-define expectations and provide a sense of security. Since a child with ADHD likely doesn't have much of an innate sense for organization, they must observe and experience organization to learn this skill. This is best accomplished by creating a structured (organized) environment for them and modeling planning and organization skills.

Create Your Schedule

There are certain activities that will definitely be a consistent part of your schedule when parenting a child with ADHD. These include doctor visits, behavioral therapy, and possibly occupational therapy. As well, you should meet with your child's teacher at least a couple of times a school year to discuss how they are doing academically and adjust their accommodations accordingly.

There are many additional things that *should* be a part of your regular schedule when raising a child with ADHD, too.

Outside Play

> A routine and predictable schedule pre-define expectations and provide a sense of security.

Applied Psychology: Health and Well-Being published a study on outdoor play in a green environment and its effects on ADHD in 2011. They found that children who had routine outdoor time in a green setting had milder ADHD symptoms than their counterparts with ADHD who didn't[6].

Be sure your child has outdoor playtime in a green setting on a consistent basis — once or twice daily is ideal.

Exercise

Exercise, as little as twenty minutes, can improve focus according to a study conducted at the University of Michigan and published in *The Journal of Pediatrics* in 2012. Half the participants used a treadmill for twenty minutes and then took reading comprehension tests. The other half just took the test. The children who exercised before the test performed better[7]. Ideally, your child will get twenty or more minutes of sustained exercise before going to school each day. This could be a morning dance party, a walk through your neighborhood, jumping on a trampoline, or even a couple of rounds of an activity on Wii Sports, which would fulfill this need. Make exercise routine for your child with ADHD and you will see benefits.

Chores

A consistent commitment to chores will be a benefit to your child, and to you. Children need to experience that it takes contribution from everyone to make a community (i.e., a family) run smoothly. They also need to learn to take responsibility for themselves. Be sure to choose tasks that are age- and maturity-appropriate. My son was responsible for setting the table when he was young. Now that he is twelve, he is also responsible for emptying the dishwasher each day. Your child will baulk at first, but chores will become habit, potentially setting them up for success when they are on their own, too. A very helpful chore for families with one or more members with ADHD is a nightly quick pick-up. Before going to bed (this can be part of your child's bedtime routine), each person is responsible for picking up their items around the house and putting them away *where they belong*. This keeps the mess from getting so large that it is too overwhelming for your child to handle on their own. This also reinforces organization skills.

Sensory Activities

It is helpful to create a sensory diet for kids with ADHD who also have sensory issues (which is a large percentage of kids with ADHD). This should be part of one of your consistent routines or on your schedule regularly. Activities from your child's sensory diet should take place four to seven days a week, but daily is ideal.

> **Sensory Seekers**: Ricochet has sensory processing disorder (SPD), sometimes also referred to as Sensory Integration Disorder (SID), in addition to ADHD. Kids with SPD are either sensory avoiders or sensory seekers, for the most part. Ricochet is most definitely a sensory seeker — he has bounced through life like Tigger since the age of three. However, he also has a few sensory sensitivities, like loud noises and tags and seams in his clothing. I came to realize that sensory-seeking behaviors — jumping, fidgeting,

chewing, flailing arms, and crashing into things on purpose — can also be a part of ADHD, too. ADHD, in simplest terms, is a deficit of sensory stimulation in the brain, the stimulation that keeps the brain alert and focused. When Ricochet needs to remain focused and still, his bodily movements are ramped up and exaggerated, and often inappropriate for the situation. Through doing heavy-work exercises before a task that requires a great deal of concentration (like reading a chapter book), he gets the sensory stimulation he needs without potentially interrupting his activity with wild and exaggerated movements. Lindsey Biel, OTR/L and Nancy Peske recommend in their book, *Raising a Sensory Smart Child*, that you work with an occupational therapist to accurately create and calibrate a sensory diet for your child[8]. Sometimes it can be tough to tell if a child is over-stimulated or under-stimulated in their reactions to sensory stimuli. Below is a sample list of activities good for sensory-seekers, but consult your child's occupational therapist (OT) to create their custom sensory diet.

> Bear hugs

> Jump on a "crash pad," jump rope, or do jumping jacks

> Lie under a weighted blanket

> Manipulate therapy putty or other resistant clay

> Dance

> Bounce on a hop-it ball

> Push something heavy like a shopping cart or a loaded wheelbarrow

> Carry heavy objects, like a stack of books or a loaded shopping bag

› Listen to loud music or music with an intense beat

› Bang on pots and pans or drums

› Eat crunchy foods

› Chew gum

› Suck thick liquid (like a milk shake) through a straw

› **Sensory Avoiders:** Some children with SPD are sensory avoiders — they are sensory-sensitive and become easily over-stimulated. Your child might be experiencing sensory-overload if they put their hands over their eyes or ears, begin rocking back and forth, or start to panic. A sensory diet is very effective for sensory avoiders as well. Again, be sure to seek the advice of your child's OT to structure and calibrate the sensory diet appropriately. Ricochet is sensitive to sounds, tags and seams in clothing (tactile), swinging, and hanging upside-down. Occupational therapy helped him immensely with his aversion to swinging because they pushed him a little further with it on different types of swings each week until that sensitivity had greatly improved over time. He also tried Tomatis therapy (a listening therapy) for his audiological sensitivity, but without success. I take noise-cancelling headphones with me for any activities where I know the sound level will be loud, such as fireworks. Below is a list of sensory activities to help children who are sensory sensitive and become easily over-stimulated. Again, consult your OT to create your child's tailored sensory diet. Constructing an effective sensory diet for a sensory-avoider is much more difficult because it requires slowly and carefully leading them into activities they have an aversion to, but without making them too uncomfortable, which is tricky.

> Gentle massage or back rub

> Rocking

> Water play or swimming (unless they have an aversion to water)

> Listen to soft, soothing music, white noise, or gentle nature sounds

> Turn the lights low and have quiet time

> Look at photos

> Lick a lollipop

> Swing gently

Create Routines

For our purposes, routines are different from your schedule, but will be part of your schedule. Create routines for the regular activities that require multiple steps — for instance, a bedtime routine or a morning routine. Most of us don't think about it, but there are many, many steps to getting ready for bed. As I suggested prior, start with the quick pick-up. Once that's done, they need to take off their clothes, put on their pajamas, and put their dirty clothes in the laundry basket. Then they have to use the restroom, brush their teeth, rinse with mouthwash, and possibly wash their face. After that, it's probably time for reading, tuck-in, and lights out. That's eleven steps in its most generic form. To our kids' brains, it's at least triple that because all of the steps I outlined are each really a multi-step neurological process. Talk about overwhelming!

Kids with ADHD aren't simply going to remember this routine because you spoke it to them once, twice, or even a hundred times. You must post the steps as a reminder and a guide. Add pictures for each item for younger kids, those who struggle with reading, or those who respond better to visuals.

I created a checklist for the morning routine when Ricochet was younger. I typed it in a large font on a four-by-six sheet of paper and laminated it simply with self-adhesive photo laminating pockets. The checklist had a paperclip on the side to mark Ricochet's place in the list and to slide down as he made progress with his tasks. The last step was a reward — time to play electronics if he finished the list by a certain time (the time we used was twenty minutes before we had to leave the house for school).

Morning Routine: RICOCHET
- ☐ Get dressed
- ☐ Pajamas in dirty clothes basket
- ☐ Brush teeth
- ☐ Swish mouth wash
- ☐ Make breakfast choice
- ☐ Make lunch choice
- ☐ Eat Breakfast

☆ If complete before 7:20 am and breakfast is eaten, you may use electronics.

The card with the clip felt like a game to him, and the immediate reward at the end motivated him to finish the routine. This type of checklist can be created for any multi-step task that occurs regularly for your child. The list can be posted on the wall where it will be used, or be designed to be carried from place-to-place to follow along. Most lists need to be mobile because all tasks on the list won't be completed in the same location.

Following is a list of potential activities you can create a step-by-step visual routine for:

> morning routine

> bedtime routine

> homework time

> chores (a list for all chores or multiple checklists, one for each chore)

> taking care of your pets

> washing the dog

> cleaning the guinea pig cage

> cleaning your room

> washing the car

> emptying the litter box

> etc.

I challenge you to make gratitude part of your bedtime routine as well (or part of another routine that occurs every day, if a different time will work better for your family). When dealing with challenges on a regular basis, it's important to keep perspective and end every day on a positive note. Before your kids head to bed, have them write one thing they're

When dealing with challenges on a regular basis, it's important to keep perspective and end every day on a positive note.

grateful for in a family gratitude journal (parents should participate, too). If they struggle with writing, record it for them — you want this activity to be pleasurable, not a chore. Be careful not to judge the quality of their gratitude. If they are grateful for the new toy they got that day instead of having a roof over their heads, that's okay. The point of this exercise is to reframe everyone's thoughts back to the positive at the end of the day, not to teach them what is really important in life.

I tell Ricochet something positive every night when I tuck him in. It usually starts with, "I like the way you…" I try to choose something that he is working on improving that I saw him doing well that day, or I compliment something I love about him...

"I like the way you let your friend choose the activity when he was at our house today."

"I like the way you told Momma the truth when the vase was broken."

"I like the way you said 'Excuse me, please' and then waited for me to finish talking to Daddy before you started talking."

"I like the way you ate your snack at the table and not in the living room."

"I like the way you let me know where you were going before you went outside to play."

"I like the way you were concerned when your friend was sad and you tried to help her laugh and feel better."

Not only does this end the day on a positive note for Ricochet, but he usually falls asleep with a smile. I also get a reminder of his strengths and all he does right/well to close my day. This is the simplest little thing really, but it makes a monumental positive impact.

Publish Your Schedule & Routines

Kids with ADHD do best in a predictable and consistent environment. Posting your schedule at least a week at a time allows them to reference it whenever they want. They can look at the calendar to know what to expect throughout each day or to find out how long until a highly-anticipated activity that's on the horizon. This will reduce the amount of times you hear, "What are we doing next?" or, "How long until we [go swimming]?" Your sanity will be a little more intact, your child's anxiety will decrease, and your child will learn independence, all from simply posting your weekly schedule. This tip is so easy, but packs a big punch in benefits.

I have used family-style calendars for this with success — both a dry-erase and the Post-It version. (Look out for kids discreetly erasing and making changes if you use a dry-erase calendar though.) The key is to hang your family calendar where everyone can see it anytime they want. This doesn't have to be the actual calendar you use to keep your own life on track — I'm not asking you to ~~jump in the deep end~~ give up your system; this family calendar can just be a copy, a reference posted for your kids.

Each time you complete the display calendar for the upcoming week, gather up your children (and your spouse too, if needed) and go through the week's events together. What I like about the structure of the family calendar is that our kids can find their row or column of the calendar and see their events distinctly, but they can also compare them to see who else in the family will be with them at a certain time or when someone might be out of town or the like. Knowing these things in advance helps kids feel safe and secure.

Another benefit of posting the schedule is teaching our children planning and organization, two sets of skills that aren't inherent for most individuals with ADHD. By creating and reviewing the schedule together, you are modeling successful planning and organization for your kids, and they will internalize those experiences as skills over time. As with just about everything when parenting a child with ADHD, be consistent — stick to this system and you will eventually see results. Lasting change takes time.

How to Handle a Change in Schedule or Routine

If you know of a change to your schedule or routine early enough, you can make the change on your posted family schedule and talk about it with your child. They will be disappointed, but you can talk them through it and teach them the skills to get themselves through disappointment and unexpected changes. For example, Ricochet was really looking forward to meeting some friends at the pool on Friday. But on Wednesday, I found out we'd have to postpone it to the following week. He was quite upset at first, but we talked about how he was still going to see his friends and he was still going swimming. We looked at the calendar and saw the date when we would meet them the following week. We talked about how things change sometimes without our control, but we still have the power to make it work out in the end. He was disappointed for a short time, and then he went on — no meltdown.

Last-minute changes are much, much tougher. Most children with ADHD don't have the skills to manage frustration

> *Empathy is a fundamental tool in successfully parenting a child with ADHD.*

appropriately. They often can't see any other option but the one they had planned either. You must teach your children these skills that are lagging. The best way to do that is to teach them to problem-solve by talking through a problem together to reach a solution, each and every time.

Here's an example: When Ricochet was in first grade, he went to his former school every Thursday afternoon to play with his friend while his sister attended her Girl Scout meeting. We had followed this routine in schedule every week for about eight months by this time. One week his friend wasn't there, and we couldn't stay either because the girls were making Mother's Day surprises. Ricochet had a complete and utter meltdown, and it ruined the entire rest of the day. He was so frustrated and disappointed and simply couldn't focus on the fact that all would be back to normal the following week. The entire family repeatedly suffered the effects of his lagging frustration tolerance the rest of that day.

As he's grown older and matured, he can now handle a majority of these situations with success, with my help. Here's the way I would handle the same situation today:

> *Children need to know that their feelings matter, that they have been heard, and that they can take some control over the situation when their emotions become overwhelming.*

"Ricochet, Buddy, we are not going to be able to stay here and play today like you usually do. Let's go find something else fun to do," I'd say in a gentle, calm tone.

He'd likely respond, "No! I only want to play with my friend! On Thursdays I get to play with him. I don't get to see him any other time."

"I understand how you feel. I know you are disappointed that you can't stay and play with your friend today. Feeling frustrated is normal when this sort of thing happens. I feel frustrated about things I can't control sometimes, too. When will you see him next?" I'll ask.

"Next week… but that's too long! I can't wait that long!" Ricochet would still be frustrated, but would be feeling secure because I let him know that I understood how he was feeling.

"Yes, Sweetie, you can. You wait that long all the time. I know you are disappointed, but let's turn that around and do something fun until we have to come back and pick up Warrior Girl. What would you like to do?"

He'd probably list several crazy things that can't be done on a whim or in an hour, but I would help him with reasonable ideas too, and we'd choose something together. *Empathy is a fundamental tool in successfully parenting a child with ADHD.* Children need to know that their feelings matter, that they have been heard, and that they can take some control over the situation when their emotions become overwhelming.

The scenario above happened when Ricochet was six. Today, at twelve years old, he hasn't had a meltdown over a sudden change in schedule but a few times in at least a year or two, and none as big as The Great Girls Scouts Meltdown of 2009, now emblazoned in my memory. Growing maturity and self-awareness play a role in that, but the biggest influence is that I have been empathetic and I guide him through problem-solving and thinking things through every time there's an opportunity. It took about a year of using that process to get to the point where we could prevent most meltdowns due to an unexpected change in schedule, but we did get there, and you can, too. Notice, I didn't say I got to a point where I could prevent all meltdowns — that's just not possible with low frustration tolerance and hyper-emotional sensitivity — but I can prevent many meltdowns now, and a sudden change in schedule is one we do pretty well with five years later.

CREATE ROUTINES

Here are some routine checklists you may copy and use with your child. For a digital version you can customize, visit http://WhatToExpectADHD.com/forms-and-checklists/. These cards are 4x6 inches so you can laminate them with the self-adhesive pouches available at most craft and office supply stores.

_____'s Morning Checklist

☐ Eat breakfast

☐ Take your medicine

☐ Get dressed

☐ Put your dirty pajamas in the laundry

☐ Brush your teeth and swish

　　mouthwash

☐ Pack your backpack

☐ Put your socks and shoes on

If you're finished by _____ AM, you can

_____.

Great job! ☺

CREATE ROUTINES

It's Homework Time

☐ Get your homework and materials from your backpack

☐ Get a pencil and sharpen it

☐ Grab any other supplies that you need to complete today's homework

☐ Find a quiet, comfortable place to work

☐ Ask for help if you need it

☐ Put your materials away and your homework in your backpack when finished

Great job! ☺

CREATE **ROUTINES**

How to Clean Your Room

☐ Gather dirty clothes and put them in

the hamper

☐ Put away large toys

☐ Put away small toys

☐ Make your bed

☐ Dust the surfaces

☐ Vacuum the floor

Great
job! ☺

CREATE ROUTINES

_____'s Bedtime Checklist

- ☐ Do a quick tidy
- ☐ Put on your pajamas
- ☐ Put your dirty clothes in the hamper
- ☐ Brush your teeth
- ☐ Use the bathroom
- ☐ Choose a book to read
- ☐ Snuggle into bed

Great job! ☺

Step 4: Get to Know Your Child

>>>>>>>>>

"When people talk, listen completely. Most people never listen."
—Ernest Hemingway

Yes, I know, you *"know"* your child. Now you must get to know them in a meaningful way as it relates to their ADHD and other challenges. It is vital to your child's future and your parenting success to uncover their triggers, strengths and weaknesses, sensory sensitivities, other co-occurring conditions (like learning disabilities or anxiety), and more. You will get to know your child with ADHD on a deeper level than most parents know their children, and there are some key strategies for doing so.

First, you must strive to understand what it feels like to have ADHD — to truly and accurately put yourself in your child's shoes. Grace Friedman, author of *Embracing Your ADHD*, and founder of addyteen.com, describes life with ADHD with an analogy that we can all visualize and embrace: "Explaining what it is like to have ADHD is like describing the scent of a rose to someone who has never seen a flower," says Friedman. "Envision this: five teens line up to race the 1,000 meters. Four of them wear shorts and sneakers and the fifth is wearing a hazmat suit and a 30-pound backpack. It should not surprise anyone that the fifth runner will not likely outpace the others. Now imagine the hazmat suit and the 30-pound backpack are transparent/invisible — that is what it is like to have ADHD. Kids with ADHD often feel ashamed, stigmatized, embarrassed, and isolated. Everyone wonders why we are not the fastest runners. I am a runner with the backpack and I know I may never outpace my peers, but I have to run anyway — life requires it." Revisit this visual each time it feels like your child lacks motivation or isn't trying hard enough. Remember the added weight and disadvantage under which they operate.

> *Truly and accurately put yourself in your child's shoes.*

Second, determine your child's developmental age and reference it as your new yardstick when defining expectations and creating routines for them. This is *not* the number of years since your child was born. Their developmental age is the age that correlates with their current social, emotional, and intellectual stage. Most kids with ADHD have a developmental age two to three years behind their chronological age; e.g., if your child with ADHD is nine years old, their developmental age is likely only six or seven. There's a big difference in parental expectations for a seven-year-old versus a nine-year-old. It's difficult, but you have to shift your thinking when considering your child's age.

Third, you know your child's personality, his likes and dislikes, and his favorite foods. Now it's time to learn why he always has a meltdown at the grocery store, what motivates him to do his homework, or why he has a fit every morning when it's time to put on his shoes. When something is off kilter with your child, take the time to reflect on the situation and make a plan for a different outcome next time they are in a similar situation or have similar feelings about something. I am a firm believer that there's always an answer to the question "Why?" if we look hard enough. Your job right now is to study your child with ADHD and discover their particular whys.

Get to know your child in a meaningful way as it relates to their ADHD by employing the following techniques:

Meltdown vs. Temper Tantrum

There's a big difference between a temper tantrum and a meltdown. When a child is having a temper tantrum, they are throwing a fit to get what they want. During a tantrum, a child will not hurt themselves and the behavior can stop in an instant as if controlled by a switch. If ignored, a tantrum will end.

A meltdown is seen in kids on the autism spectrum, including kids with ADHD. A meltdown can be triggered by frustration, anxiety, or sensory overload. A tantrum from a child on the spectrum can, and often does, turn into a meltdown. There is a complete loss of self-control during a meltdown, and the child will not be able to consider the safety of themselves or others. Unlike a tantrum, a meltdown must cycle and will taper off slowly — it's as though their brain has been hijacked. There's nothing you can do or say to stop a meltdown once it has started.

Understanding this distinction between a temper tantrum and a meltdown is vital to your parenting success, of course, but also to your child's self-esteem. Be sure everyone in your child's life is aware of the difference. My son was once forced to apologize to his entire fourth grade class for having a "temper tantrum" when he actually had a meltdown (induced by his teacher's rigidity and lack of understanding of his special needs). The staff could have used this teachable moment to educate his peers about differences, but myths were perpetuated instead, and my son endured extreme embarrassment, shame, and social harm. Needless to say, this momma threw a tantrum of her own after hearing about it — to the teacher, principal, and the head of special education for the entire county.

A child has intent when having a tantrum, but cannot control their behavior in the depths of a meltdown.

Keep a Daily Journal

It's important to keep a detailed journal for at least the first year after your child's ADHD diagnosis and starting treatment. Recording symptoms, activities, meltdowns, food intake, sleep, vitamins, medication, etc., will provide the opportunity to reflect and make adjustments where necessary for better outcomes in the future.

Everyone has individual reactions to particular things or events. I was terrified about riding in an elevator until I was in my twenties — true story! My biggest fear was that the doors would close on someone. My fear frustrated my parents when I was a child and caused me a lot of anxiety for many years as well. I tried to conquer the fear and finally remembered that I had seen

Every child with ADHD is unique in their differences and struggles.

a little bit of a movie in the early 1980s where a woman was running from someone trying to hurt her and the elevator door closed on her leg but the elevator went up anyway. I saw it when I was about seven years old, when I got out of bed one evening to talk to my parents. They didn't realize I saw this fictitious event, or that it scared me, and I wasn't old enough to recognize and articulate this causation, so my fear of elevators seemed to come out of nowhere for my parents, yet there was a very logical explanation under the surface.

These are the types of cause-and-effect scenarios you want to uncover so you can improve their outcomes for your child with ADHD. When your child has a behavior outburst or a full meltdown, afterwards write down the who/what/when/where of the situation before, during, and after the episode. Who were they with when it started to go downhill? Where were they during that time? What were they doing when it began and just prior? What time of day did the outburst occur? What was the outburst like? Then analyze this data to try to figure out what could have triggered the unwanted outcome.

Discovering Triggers

Developing a causal map of our children's complexities is crucial when parenting a child with ADHD. Guiding them through problem solving teaches them the skills necessary to cope with their difficulties instead of breaking down or shutting down.

Use the data you record in your daily journal to discover what triggers your child's inappropriate reactions, unwanted behavior, and meltdowns. When I first realized that my son had no concept of time, many of his prior upsets made more sense. He would become distraught when I told him we would go to the park in three hours because three hours felt like an eternity to him — he had no concept of when in his vast future that time would finally come. When I identified that trigger, I was able to reframe my conversations with him about time-related subjects in a way he could better understand and which made him feel more secure, and that reduced his whining and nagging in most of these instances.

Ricochet also lives in the moment — he can't see any other way but the scenario in his mind at one particular instant, although this skill has improved immensely in the last year (four years after diagnosis and treatment began). If I told him his neighborhood friend wasn't available to play today, he would get disproportionately upset for the circumstances. Once I realized he only saw one option in his way of thinking, playing *today*, I was able to adjust my delivery of this type of information for him. Now I'd say, "Your neighbor friend can't play today after all, but let's make a plan with him for after lunch tomorrow instead." The addition of that one extra phrase seems so simple, but we don't think about the need for it because common sense tells us that it's obvious there is always another day to play. For Ricochet, that additional few words I added when breaking the news of a change in schedule reminded him that there is another day they can get together, many other days in fact. That reminder allowed him to see that his plans were just postponed, not cancelled forever. He was still disappointed and upset about it, because tomorrow seems so far away in his universe, but he didn't have a meltdown over it. I know it sounds like a lot of extra work to choose your words and delivery of information so carefully for something seemingly trivial and simple, but it's neither trivial nor simple in your child's brain.

Every child with ADHD is unique in their differences and struggles — what triggers a meltdown in my child may not bother your child at all, and vice-versa. However, most children with ADHD are trailing behind their peers with some core skills, and these lagging skills are often the culprit when looking for triggers. Here is a list of some common triggers to watch for:

> Low frustration tolerance

> Poor sense of time, sometimes referred to as time-blindness

> Feeling like they don't have any control over their life and what happens to them

> Concrete thinking — they see black and white, but no grey; they don't understand analogies and figures of speech. (I once said to Ricochet, under my breath, "You're going to be the death of me," and he thought that literally meant he was going to kill me. As he has gotten older, he has finally begun to recognize that not everything is

literal, but he still struggles greatly with the distinction without help interpreting.)

> Feeling like they can't do anything right

> Feeling like they are not being heard (this is where empathy is so key)

> Sensory sensitivities or sensory overload (like the lump of the seams in the toe of your socks, the tag in your shirt poking the back of your neck, or a loud, chaotic environment)

If you haven't yet, pick up and read *The Explosive Child* by Dr. Ross Greene, and visit his website at LivesintheBalance.org. Your child doesn't have to be explosive for you to get a great number of benefits from reading this book. I learned about lagging skills and problem solving with Ricochet from Dr. Greene's books, and it changed our lives.

Study Their Positive Traits

It's vitally important to talk about more than just our child's weaknesses and struggles, whether we are talking to our child directly, to someone else while our child can hear us, or to any others in their lives. If we spend all our time talking about ADHD, life becomes all about ADHD, and that leaves no room for anything else. As parents of kids with ADHD, we owe it to them to help them discover and nurture their talents and interests. Self-confidence can't be instilled in an environment where conversations and activities always revolve around ADHD and weaknesses.

You made a list of everything good about your child in *Step 1: Get Over It*. Review that list and add to it now. Even the small things count here. Be sure your list includes their strengths, talents, hobbies, aptitudes, positive personality traits, athleticism, interests, etc... Really go the extra mile to fill a page. Ask your child to join you and help you fill the list. Talking about their positive traits is one of the very best things you can do for your child.

My list of strengths for Ricochet:
- Kind
- Gentle
- Considerate
- Loyal
- Good at math
- Good at science
- Loves chemistry and physics
- Very smart
- Enormously creative
- Charming
- Good with animals
- Intuitive with technology
- Approachable
- Loves graphic novels
- Great at video games
- Interested in how things work
- Loves to explore
- Tenacious
- Witty
- Enjoys making others laugh
- Determined

Once you complete your list of wonderfulness, ask your child to help you pick two items on the list that they would like to do more of or learn more about. For instance, if your child is into mechanics and how things work, offer to sign him up for a kid's electrical circuitry class or purchase a kit for children to experiment with mechanics at home (the website ToysAreTools.com is an excellent resource for toys that are science-based and inspire thoughtful play). Or if he's really into working with clay, offer to enroll him in pottery classes, or get some clay and tools for a little home pottery studio. Ricochet has participated in several summer day camps that focused on science and did well with all of them because he is super-interested in the subject.

When our kids have opportunities to do things well and succeed often, they begin to realize they aren't just "a screw-up," "stupid," "lazy," or any number of other negative things kids with ADHD often think about themselves when they perpetually hear about their weaknesses, or

If we spend all our time talking about ADHD, life becomes all about ADHD and that leaves no room for anything else.

when they can't ever seem to reach the level of their peers. Facilitate excitement about the things your child with ADHD excels in — the rewards will be exponentially greater than the investment and will last a lifetime.

DAILY JOURNAL

It is important to track the efficacy of treatment, whether that includes medication, supplements, or a particular diet. Use these charts daily to record how your child is responding to treatment. Be sure to take the journal with you to every doctor and therapy appointment. This data will help your child's care provider determine the efficacy of each portion of treatment and discover interactions or other red flags.

DATE
/ /

Monday | Tuesday | Wednesday | Thursday | Friday | Saturday | Sunday

MEDICATION

NAME & DOSE

☐ BRAND   ☐ GENERIC

TIME GIVEN

____ : ____

☐ AM ☐ PM

NAME & DOSE

☐ BRAND   ☐ GENERIC

TIME GIVEN

____ : ____

☐ AM ☐ PM

SUPPLEMENT _____ Brand _____ Dose _____ Time __ : __

SUPPLEMENT _____ Brand _____ Dose _____ Time __ : __

SLEEP

WOKE UP

____ : ____

☐ AM ☐ PM

FELL ALSEEP

____ : ____

☐ AM ☐ PM

wake during the night?
☐ yes ☐ no

Any additional sleep today? ____ hours

When? _____

FOOD

FOOD EATEN TODAY (WITH CORRESPONDING TIMES)

BREAKFAST ___:___   SNACK ___:___   LUNCH ___:___   SNACK ___:___   DINNER ___:___   SNACK ___:___

BEHAVIOR

NEGATIVE BEHAVIORS WITH TIMES

POSITIVE BEHAVIORS WITH TIMES

ANALYZE OUTBURSTS

Uncover cause-and-effect scenarios so you can improve outcomes for your child with ADHD. When your child has a behavior outburst or a full meltdown, complete this chart once chart once everyone is calm. Then analyze this data to figure out what may have triggered the outburst.

1. Label the outburst
2. Describe the details

	OUTBURST/ MELTDOWN	OUTBURST/ MELTDOWN
CONTEXT / CIRCUMSTANCES *Who/When/Where*		
ANTECEDENT (What was going on just before?) *Why*		
BEHAVIOR *What*		
CONSEQUENCE (What happened after?)		
COMMENTS AND OTHER OBSERVATIONS		
POSSIBLE TRIGGERS		

IMPORTANT!

NURTURE THEIR GIFTS AND INTERESTS

Copy two or three of your child's positive traits, interests, and talents that you want to support and nurture from the Focus on the Positive Worksheet (Step 1, page 25). Use the chart below to develop and record your plan to nurture these gifts and interests. Make a copy of this page so you can utilize this chart in the future for other focuses, or as their interests change and develop.

POSITIVE TRAITS, INTERESTS, OR TALENTS

Describe ideas to nurture this gift, interest, or talent

1

2

3

4

FINAL PLAN OF ACTION

Step 5: Make a Plan

"A goal without a plan is just a wish."

—Antoine de Saint-Exupéry

Use all that you've discovered about your child's ADHD complexities in *Step 4: Get to Know Your Child* to formulate a plan for positive change. Parents of children with ADHD must adjust their expectations and reframe their perspective to measure their child by a different yardstick, not the standard measurement guide meant for their neurotypical peers. Now it's time to reference the list of triggers you compiled in *Step 4: Get to Know Your Child* to intervene when times get rough, and utilize your newfound knowledge of your child's true strengths and weaknesses to make a plan to appropriately shape their future. We're going to assemble all of this information now to create your plan to modify your child's inappropriate behaviors and improve life for them, and the whole family.

Define Expectations

Kids want rules. As much as they contest it, it's true: they crave rules. They want to know where their boundaries are, whether they realize it consciously or not. They need to see these barrier lines both to stay within them to do the right thing and please us, and to push them and overstep them when they feel like ~~getting in trouble~~ garnering (negative) attention or making a statement. We have a human need to have clearly-defined expectations, and kids aren't immune to that, especially kids with ADHD.

A simple system of routine checklists (as discussed in *Step 3: Create Structure*) often works because the checklists provide kids with consistent and clearly-defined expectations — they know undoubtedly when they'll be rewarded and when they'll be punished.

The structure of defining expectations removes anxiety and provides room for calm as well. Imagine you are given a verbal command to stay within "your area." If there's a chalk outline on the floor around you, you feel pretty good that you can stay within that area — you know where the boundaries are, and you are comfortable with the task. But if you are asked to stay within "your area" and there are no visible boundaries,

> The structure of defining expectations removes anxiety and provides room for calm.

nor instructions to define the boundaries of "your area," you are likely to feel anxious about being able to comply with this task. You will be uncomfortable not knowing if you are successfully working toward your goal. The power of clearly defined expectations is noticeably logical. Of course, adding a reward at the end further encourages successful completion of the task.

Don't assume a child with ADHD knows their boundaries for any given task. Yes, sometimes the boundaries are common sense, but common sense isn't always intuitive for a child with ADHD. Err on the side of defining too much rather than too little, and you will see the benefits of clearly-defined expectations in your family, too.

> *Don't assume a child with ADHD knows their boundaries for any given task. Yes, sometimes the boundaries are common sense, but common sense isn't always intuitive for a child with ADHD.*

Create and Post House Rules

A physical list of house rules is another way to clearly define expectations for children. Posting the list in your home removes any doubt about the overarching guidelines and when they are met or broken. Your house rules are the law of the land for your home and your family. If the law is broken, there will be consequences — that explanation is simple for kids with ADHD to visualize and understand.

Always write rules from an actionable perspective: "Do _____." Do not state rules by starting with negative phrasing: "Do not _____." Your list of house rules might include:

> › Speak kindly to others
>
> › Give lots of hugs
>
> › If you take it out, you put it away
>
> › Respect everyone's belongings and private spaces
>
> › Laugh often
>
> › Apologize when you were wrong
>
> › Show compassion for others

> Count to ten slowly before showing your anger

> Use your words to convey how you feel

> *Tell* others how you feel when you're upset, but *show* others how you feel when you are happy

> Keep your promises

> Tell the truth

> Ask permission before you leave the house

> If you don't know, ask

> Listen when others are talking

> Admit your mistakes

> Speak to others without whining

> When you decide to do something, give it your all

> Dream big

> Help others often

> Play outside often

> Complete your chores without complaining

It doesn't matter how you compile and display the house rules, as long as the list is legible to everyone (use pictures as well as text for young kids and those who don't read well) and in a central location in your home where everyone in the family will see them often. It helps to be able to reference them when reminding your child of the rules or discussing consequences.

Address Triggers

In *Step 4: Get to Know Your Child*, you learned how to discover your child's triggers by keeping a journal and being resolutely observant when upset happens. It's time to take the triggers data you've been gathering and use it to affect change for your child and your family.

First, review the list of triggers with your child and how that particular trigger makes them feel. For example:

TRIGGERS IDENTIFIED:

> Low frustration tolerance

> Feeling like they don't have any control over their life and what happens to them

TELL YOUR CHILD:

"I know you get really frustrated when something you were looking forward to is cancelled or postponed. Can you tell me what that feels like to you?"

As you talk to them about these challenges, which they no doubt want to change as much as you do, listen for clues. They may be able to tell you how they are feeling when this particular trigger occurs. Or, they may give you other clues to increase your awareness of when they are being triggered in this way, which will clue you in to offer assistance and coaching to appropriately handle the situation.

A trigger can be something that happens, usually out of the child's control, such as postponing an activity they were looking forward to. Or, a trigger could be sensory overload — a noisy or chaotic environment. A trigger could also be someone's tone of voice when they spoke to your child. Triggers are environmental, social, and/or cognitive. They are different for each individual, which is why it is so important to be observant each time your child struggles. You will use this knowledge to reshape and improve your child's reactions.

Addressing Troublesome Behavior at School

If your child struggles with frequent inappropriate and disruptive behaviors at school, request a Functional Behavior Assessment (FBA) from your school system. A Behavioral Specialist will facilitate a meeting with your child's teachers (and hopefully you) and complete the assessment in order to produce viable strategies for improvement. The team will:

> › *list troubling behaviors,*
>
> › *note the frequency, intensity, and duration of each behavior,*
>
> › *specify what each behavior looks like (for example, 'Ricochet begins clenching his teeth'),*
>
> › *define what perceived function the behavior may serve for the child,*
>
> › *brainstorm what skill deficits are related to the behavior,*
>
> › *and, most importantly, determine strategies to employ to reduce the frequency and intensity of the problem behavior.*

The FBA process will likely include a few light-bulb moments for your child's teachers and will provide great insight to your child's behaviors in general. Of course, implementation of strategies in the classroom will determine if the intended efficacy of the FBA process is met.

Change Reactions

Triggers set off a reaction, plain and simple — it's cause and effect. In a child with ADHD, these reactions can be disproportionate to the situation and/or undesirable. To modify these behavioral outcomes, we have to teach our children the skills necessary to enable them to change their reactions to their

104

triggers. Some triggers can be avoided, while others we just have to make and implement a plan to handle, hunker down, and get through.

Environmental

Environmental triggers can often be confronted and managed. If there's a loud or chaotic store your child struggles with, don't take him into that store, or keep your time there to a minimum. If bright light makes your child uncomfortable, consider that and what you can do to accommodate it before entering that kind of environment. Take note of the similarities of the environments your child struggles with, and limit their time under those environmental circumstances.

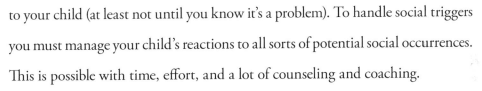

Social

Social triggers are a little more difficult to influence. You often don't have control over what someone says to your child or their tone when speaking to your child (at least not until you know it's a problem). To handle social triggers you must manage your child's reactions to all sorts of potential social occurrences. This is possible with time, effort, and a lot of counseling and coaching.

In second grade, Ricochet would punch anyone he perceived had wronged him or one of his classmates. If the student next to him cut in line, he'd punch them. If a peer said something ugly to him or one of his classmates, he'd punch them. If Sally used Johnny's yellow crayon without asking first, he'd punch her. Ricochet was the (inappropriate) sheriff of the 2nd grade. It took us about eight months of very focused behavior modification techniques to change his reaction to that trigger, feeling that someone did something wrong. Ricochet didn't have the skills to communicate that he was angry any other way than to hit the one he was angry toward. Taking a swing at someone was his natural, subconscious reaction, in the absence of intrinsic appropriate anger management skills and social knowledge.

For each and every instance that he hit another child, we started by asking him what happened to make him hit the other person. It was always that they had made him mad, broken the rules, or weren't kind. Next, I asked him to give me appropriate alternative behaviors — to name acceptable ways to communicate that he was angry. We would discuss three or four options such as: tell the teacher, use words to tell the person you didn't like what they did, walk away, etc. After talking about acceptable reactions, I asked him if hitting was one of the appropriate ideas we discussed. Nope, hitting is not a suitable way to express your anger.

The conversation went something like this:

Momma: "Ricochet, why did you hit Sally?"

Ricochet: "She took Johnny's yellow crayon without even asking! Ms. Glenda said taking something without asking is against the rules!"

Momma: "Is it okay to hit someone?"

Ricochet: "No." (He looks down at the floor in despair.)

Momma: "What are some more appropriate ways to handle your frustration when someone breaks the rules?"

Ricochet: "I could tell my teacher."

Momma: "Yeah, that's a good one. What else?"

Ricochet: "I could tell Johnny it's not nice to take things that belong to other people without asking."

Momma: "Right! Can you think of anything else?"

Ricochet: "Sometimes you tell me to ignore what other kids do, but that's hard for me."

Momma: "I know that's hard for you. You can work on that one. Was hitting the person on that list you just told me?"

Ricochet: "No."

Momma: "Remember these new ideas we talked about whenever you are feeling frustrated or angry. Tell a grown-up you need help if you feel like hitting again. Okay?"

Ricochet: "I will, Momma."

He had several disciplinary write-ups that school year but, by the end of second grade, he was using words instead of his fists to let someone know they made him angry. In the four years since then, he's only hit one child one time, and that boy was an unrelenting bully who threw him on the ground and started punching him first.

Consistency and teaching my son options changed his instinctual reaction over time. You can use this same method to change your child's reactions to all sorts of triggers, too. Be sure you ask *your child* to suggest alternatives to the undesirable behaviors — this teaches them to problem-solve and think things through, and also gives them a feeling of control (not to mention pride).

Cognitive

I find changing reactions to cognitive triggers the toughest. These would include triggers such as not being able to figure out a math problem, not having a concept of time, not having their expectations met, or not having any control over what they have to do. The reaction to this type of trigger is simply frustration, and it's hard to change that because frustration is natural to everyone in these situations. The behavior you want to modify here isn't the initial reaction of frustration, but the secondary reaction, how they respond to the frustration. This secondary reaction can be a myriad of things from avoidance, to yelling or crying, to hurting others or themselves. And that reaction to frustration is typically more variable than you find with reactions to environmental or social triggers.

I employ the same strategy with Ricochet for managing academic frustration as I did for addressing his instinct to hit someone if they made him angry. We talk about what made him feel frustrated, why he thinks he reacted to the frustration the way he did, and appropriate alternatives to that reaction. For example, Ricochet has two learning disabilities — dysgraphia, a handwriting disorder, and written expression disorder, a difficulty getting thoughts on paper and structuring them coherently. We have completed lots of therapy and countless hours of handwriting work to no avail — we cannot "cure" his learning disabilities. As you can imagine, not being able to write legibly by sixth grade and not being able to write down the thoughts you can speak fluently to someone can be maddening. Ricochet suffers a huge amount of frustration with most writing tasks, which is the majority of each and every school day. He has an accommodation to type his work, but that only helps the dysgraphia. When he is frustrated with writing, he will show it in many different ways — avoiding the assignment, scribbling over the entire paper, tearing the paper up, crying, back-talking the teacher about doing his work, etc. Each day I know one of these things took place, I start at the beginning and walk him through alternatives for a better outcome. I always encourage him to seek help before he gets frustrated enough to act out. It's hard, but he's finally starting to do that sometimes.

You can see, whatever the trigger, the behavior modification plan to change a child's reaction requires basically the same four steps:

1. Ask your child what happened to cause their inappropriate reaction.

2. Ask your child to name appropriate alternative behaviors. It's okay to lead them to ideas if they can't come up with any on their own, but this should be a team effort if you need to help. This helps to strengthen lagging problem-solving skills.

3. Ask your child if their recent inappropriate reaction is on that list of appropriate behaviors.

4. Reiterate that the next time that particular trigger occurs, they should do one of the things on the appropriate reactions list.

Stick with it! Behavior modification is tough and takes a lot of time. Our children usually can't simply stop doing something because you told them to a ~~million~~ few times. They lack the skills to build alternatives and weigh them before acting. Behavior modification is very rewarding when you finally start seeing the benefits, so have faith in the process and keep at it.

Teach Self-Awareness

Self-awareness and self-regulation are crucially important for successful ADHD management. They create a bit of a chicken or egg dilemma — you can't have self-regulation without first having self-awareness. One must be aware of one's actions and whether or not they are appropriate before one can learn to adjust them. In my experience, self-awareness is 75 percent maturity and 25 percent skill — that means you can't just teach self-awareness, it increases as a child ages and matures. You have to wait for the egg (self-awareness) to arrive before it will hatch into a more beneficial chicken (self-regulation).

Our therapist had wanted to implement self-regulation techniques with Ricochet since he was eight years old. Each time she shared this idea, for quite a long time, I told her that he just was not ready. He seemed largely unaware of his differences and when his behavior was a problem until the summer before his ninth birthday. That's when I began to notice that he was recognizing when his behavior was problematic or something he just couldn't control.

One day soon after, he seemed to have an epiphany of self-awareness. He got very angry with me after school. We had a parent meeting with his teachers, and he wanted to go to aftercare with some of his friends instead of sit through the meeting with me. But he wasn't signed up for the aftercare program, so he needed to stay with me in the classroom. He was very frustrated that other kids could go to aftercare and he couldn't. He was overwhelmed with helplessness and began to melt down. It was a silent melt though — a lot of sulking and pushing me away, but he wasn't verbally aggressive, at least not until we got into the car and were alone.

He showed a lot of restraint in front of the teachers, and that was great progress from where we had been. We climbed into the car and he started in.

"You are the meanest mom in the world," Ricochet sputtered in his best super-mean voice. "You never, ever let me do anything I want to! You are so mean!"

Once he stopped yelling at the back of my head so I could get a word in edgewise, I tried to logically and rationally explain the situation to him.

> One must be aware of their actions and whether or not they are appropriate before they can learn to adjust them.

"I wish I could offer you all the fun things you want to experience, Buddy. I really do! But sometimes I don't have any control over what you can and can't participate in," I explained as calmly as possible. "It hurts my feelings when you get mad at me and you're mean to Momma over something I don't have the power to change." My voice was quivering a bit by the end — my emotions were welling up from the sheer exhaustion of the frequency of battles just like this one or very similar.

I was battle-weary.

After about five minutes of that back-and-forth, he fell silent and then began to cry.

"I hate it when I'm mean to people. I'm so sorry, Momma. I'm sorry I was mean to you. I hate it when I act like that," he said with a lingering whimper.

I was astonished. Of course, I cried too. I felt sad for him that he couldn't control his behavior at times — sad that it makes *him* feel so sad. I was also grateful that he was aware of what had taken place though. It was very clear he was finally aware of his differences and his actions, at least sometimes.

The approach to teach self-awareness and self-regulation is fundamentally the same system I detailed earlier, in the section on *Changing Reactions*.

1. Ask your child what was unacceptable about their behavior and what took place to cause their inappropriate reaction. You are guiding them to self-awareness after an undesirable behavior has occurred.

2. Then ask your child to list appropriate alternative behaviors for that situation or emotion. It's okay to lead them to ideas if they can't come up with any of their own, but this should be a team effort — don't just tell them what they should have done, collaborate. It is important to model the process of awareness, mindfulness, problem-solving, and regulation.

3. When they are beginning to learn self-awareness, encourage them to ask for your help, or their caregiver's help, to problem solve the next time they find themselves in a similar situation or feeling the same emotions. The caregiver can discuss the appropriate alternatives and help them remain calm enough to make good choices. Once they begin to self-regulate instinctively, they won't need to enlist help — they will just react with one of those appropriate alternatives on their own.

Emotional Sensitivity

Significant emotional sensitivity is tremendously common for those with ADHD, and it is often a trigger that gets overlooked as a co-existing mood disorder rather than part of an individual's ADHD. Dr. William W. Dodson, board-certified psychiatrist and founder of the Dodson ADHD Center, actually asks about emotional over-sensitivity as part of the diagnostic criteria when he evaluates adults for ADHD. After he completes the eighteen questions in the diagnostic manual (DSM V), he asks the following: "For your entire life have you always been much more sensitive than other people you know to rejection, teasing, criticism, or your own perception that you have failed or fallen short?"

Does that sound like your child with ADHD? *Yes. Yes! YES!* It most definitely describes mine. He always overreacts to rejection, teasing, and criticism — real or perceived. He frequently feels that the actions of his peers mean they are rejecting him, regardless of the genuine intent. For instance, just last week his neighbor friend had played with him earlier in the day and then gone home. Later, Ricochet was riding his bike and went to ask his neighbor friend if he wanted to ride bikes with him. His friend, in the middle of watching a movie, simply said, "No." Ricochet walked out his front door in tears, put his bike away in the garage, and went inside to ~~start freaking out~~ yell and slam doors because it was now a fact that his friend didn't want to play with him anymore, *ever*. His perception was not reality, but it was *Ricochet's reality*.

I talked to him about the fact that his friend isn't as high energy as he is and sometimes likes to rest and be alone in the quiet. We talked about how it doesn't mean he is not his friend anymore just because he elected not to participate in a certain activity at a certain time.

But Ricochet was wounded and, to him, it felt like a full rejection and the end of the world.

Rejection over-sensitivity is a tough creature to eliminate. To change this reaction, we have to completely reframe how our kids with ADHD process most of their social interactions — not just negative interactions — because they can often feel an innocuous action was actually an intentional rejection.

As with the prior sections I've detailed on changing reactions, improving emotional over-sensitivity takes consistent guidance and coaching to reframe a child's emotional responses. Discuss every occurrence of over-sensitivity with them, and teach them the intended message of the other's actions. This will not stick the first time, and it likely won't stick the twentieth time either. But some day in your child's future, they will hear your voice in their little subconscious voice and be more realistic in their internalizations of what others say and do to them.

Find the Discipline Balance

When you fully understand ADHD and appreciate your child's individual intricacies and challenges, you will struggle with discipline for that particular child. Expecting neurotypical behavior and punishing accordingly isn't fair when a child has a neurobehavioral disorder. But blaming every behavior on ADHD, saying, "He just can't help it," doesn't teach your child how to compensate and behave appropriately in the real world either. Defining expectations, coupled with consistent redirection, praise, and discipline, is the key to achieving an appropriate balance between discipline and ADHD.

> *His perception was not reality, but it was Ricochet's reality.*

As a compassionate parent of a child with ADHD, I really struggle with discipline. It's ironic since I had no problem being fair but firm in enforcing rules before Ricochet's diagnosis. And even after, I still had no problem doling out punishment for his neurotypical big sister, Warrior Girl, either. Rationally, discipline is easy — every action has a reaction, so every bad choice has a bad reaction, or a consequence.

When you throw ADHD into the mix though, fairness in consequences becomes ambiguous. What is a fair consequence to a child whose physiology typically prevents them from weighing consequences before taking action? Is the answer to skip consequences altogether when a child has ADHD?

That is exactly what I did for some time after Ricochet's diagnosis, I'm afraid. I allowed him to use ADHD as a crutch — an excuse for bad decisions and poor behavior. I wasn't just allowing it, *I was teaching it.* My constant response when someone attempted to punish him was, "You have to remember, he can't help it." I must have sounded like a broken record. It took some stern feedback from my husband, my virtual ADHD community, and our therapist to realize that attitude was doing Ricochet more harm than good. He quickly succumbed to learned helplessness.

So where is the balance between letting them off the hook completely and holding them to an unfair, neurotypical standard?

I've found that it's easier for me to discipline effectively, and easier for Ricochet to act appropriately and not need to be disciplined, if expectations are clearly and repeatedly defined (as discussed at the beginning of this chapter). This is one of the many times posted house rules come in handy. Your children know how they are expected to act based on the house rules. Once you've defined consequences for breaking a house rule, they know exactly what to expect each time they break the rules.

Consistency in discipline is the other key ingredient. Not just consistency yourself, but consistency among all of your child's caregivers, and that can be oh so hard.

Your children need to know the consequences for negative behaviors up front, so you must define them in advance of an action that requires punishment. For example, something on the list of pre-defined rules and expectations would result in losing screen time or something else whose possible absence will motivate appropriate behavior. A behavior you want to correct, but which isn't the worst thing in the world, could result in a less severe penalty, such as an additional small chore, or losing a bit of their allowance. Keep it minimal and keep it simple so your child can learn to mentally survey possible consequences in an instant.

Warnings are perfectly acceptable, too — in fact, they are advised if your child is not in a dangerous situation. Our therapist taught me to count to three in a very particular way for warnings of impending consequences with a child with ADHD. She advised me to use the *1-2-3 Magic* method: count down, "3-2-1" (I count backwards because I found it more effective), but count to five silently between each number to give my child with slow processing speed extra time to react to the warning.

A More Successful Way to Count Down for Kids with ADHD

State what you would like your child to do and what the consequence will be if they aren't doing it by the time you get to "one."

"That's three."

(full 5-second pause)

"That's two."

(full 5-second pause)

"That's one. Now [whatever the predetermined consequence for that behavior is]."

The simple addition of giving some time to process and react made all the difference in the world for us. Brilliant! Still today, I use this method, and Ricochet is usually compliant before I get to "one." In fact, I rarely have to count anymore. If it's not a situation where I can give a warning and count (a safety issue, for instance), he knows what the consequence will be because we set expectations and consequences for our family ahead of time.

It took some time, but I was able to undo what I'd accidentally done and teach Ricochet that ADHD is not an excuse to ~~mimic the Tasmanian devil~~ misbehave without consequence. Hopefully, you are reading this book before you unintentionally teach your child to use ADHD as a crutch, too.

At times, I fall back into this trap of using ADHD as an excuse for punishable actions. Implementing a good discipline balance despite ADHD is an ongoing parenting challenge.

Relinquish Control

It is a parent's job to maintain the control, right? We are supposed to have power over our children's behaviors to keep them safe, to teach them right from wrong, and to illustrate that there are consequences to our actions from time to time. If you received a parenting handbook when you had a baby, it would certainly have had a chapter on the importance of parental control in every parent-child relationship.

But I am throwing caution to the wind here and advising you to relinquish control to your kids, especially your kids with ADHD. Yep, give them control for once, and often.

Okay, no need to panic. I have a very good reason.

As children age and mature, they become more and more independent, typically much to their parents' dissatisfaction. They need independence to discover who they are, gain self-confidence, and learn how to meet the demands of adulthood. Remember when your child buttered their own toast for the first time? It took ~~an eternity~~ ten full minutes, and the bread was mangled once they finished, but they were beaming with pride. "Look! I did it!" Sure, you could have buttered it in twenty seconds or less without the mess and mutilation, but you wouldn't have seen that sweet expression of gratification on your kiddo's face. They discovered that they could do it for themselves, and so did you.

No doubt this is a bittersweet moment! Parents don't want their children to grow up, but they are going to do it whether we accept it or not. It's our duty to prepare them for the time when mom or dad won't be there to guide their every step and clean up both their literal and figurative messes.

There are no winners in this inevitable daily battle for control. If we parents fight for control and win, we have very angry little people to deal with. If we fight for control and let them win, we are angry and resentful and our children stop trusting that what we say has grit, moving further away from any parental control. Successful parenting requires equilibrium.

I'm not prescribing a Freaky Friday here. Instead, I propose you fake your child out a bit by offering measured choices at first, especially when they're young. When you offer a nominal number of choices, you are controlling the situation somewhat with what you offer your child to choose from, but your child feels empowered because they are making the final decision. {wink, wink}

As parents of clinically-impulsive kids, it is even harder to surrender any control to our children. {Believe me — I know!} They likely have a track record of not thinking things through before making choices. They may be oblivious to danger. But it's okay to give even the most impulsive kid some control, too; in fact, I say it's necessary. How else will they learn the universal consequences of certain actions? Making their own decisions independently also opens the door to self-confidence and control when their life with an ADHD brain often feels very much out of their control, no matter what they do.

How many of your supermarket meltdowns were because your child wanted to choose a particular cereal, but you allowed them no say in the matter? How many times have you battled in the morning to get clothes on your child before having to run out the door to school? How many times has your child refused to eat a meal because they didn't want (their favorite) food that day? All of these situations are avoidable most of the time.

Here are some ways to make your child feel empowered while still maintaining some parental control:

> Give two options of clothing for the day, and let your child pick one (it's best to do this the night before, of course). Older children should choose on their own under the parameters that their choice must be weather-appropriate and within school/family dress code. If your child doesn't care what they wear, you get a free pass — lay out their clothes each evening and do a happy dance all the way past *Go!*

> Include your child in the grocery shopping. Let them be in charge of the list and checking things off. When it's a food that's mostly for them, give them a couple of choices, where applicable, and let them make the final decision; e.g., hold up two cereal boxes and tell them they can pick one. Enlist them in reading package ingredients to police chemicals and additives you've banned from your family's diet, too. For older children, let them know you are going food shopping, ask if there's anything in particular they'd like to have, and oblige within reason.

> Get your children involved in meal planning. If you plan a weekly menu (which you should to create structure and define expectations), let your child decide which meals will fall on which days of the week. Let them choose the side dish to go with the grilled chicken when they are complaining that they'd rather have chicken nuggets. "We're having grilled chicken tonight, but I'll let you each choose a side dish to go with it. I can make green beans, baked beans, potato salad, corn on the cob,

or mashed potatoes." Take it a step further even — letting them help cook teaches valuable lessons in math and science and involves them in making nutritious choices as well, a habit you'll be glad they picked up.

› When you are on an outing — like skiing, at the beach, on a hike, or anything similar — let your child guide the activities. Allow them to decide if they want to be taught something new, or just be free to figure things out and explore. Our most enjoyable family activity is going to the beach because Ricochet can run wild and free and explore at his own pace, forcing his ADHD to the back burner. He almost always picks free play versus structured activities.

› Do you sign your children up for summer camps each year? Give them a list of camps that fit your schedule and budget, and let them choose a predetermined number of camps. They'll be most excited about participating when they decide where they'll go.

› When trying to get your child organized, get them involved in designing their organization system. This is something I learned a lot about by reading the book, *The Organized Student*. I highly recommend this book, especially to parents of middle and high school kids — the author, Donna Goldberg, makes the point time and time again throughout the book that your child must have ownership in the system, or it will fail to work for them. Even when you are purchasing their school binder, let them choose the binder they want at the store.

What choices do you give your ADHD child to help them feel more independent and in control of their world? If the answer is "not many," it's time to add more.

CREATE HOUSE RULES

Written house rules define general expectations for your household. Write them on standard notebook paper, or get creative and post them in a typographical layout like art. What matters is that you record and post them. Here are many examples of common house rules — circle the rules you want to include for your family. Keep it short. *Remember: Word all rules from a positive perspective, i.e. "Do _____," NOT "Don't _____."

When you decide to do something, give it your all!

IF YOU TAKE IT OUT, YOU PUT IT AWAY.

HeLP Others

SPEAK kindly. calmly. the truth.

KEEP YOUR PROMiSES

listen when others are talking

ask BEFORE YOU leave THE HOUSE

laugh

APOLOGIZE WHEN YOU ARE WRONG

SHOW COMPASSiON for OTHERS

DREAM BiG

TeLL others how you feeL when you're upset, but **show** others how you feeL when you are happy.

USe WORDS TO TeLL HOW YOU FeeL

Count to 10 S L O W L Y before Showing ANGER

BELiEVE in YOURSELF

TRIGGERS & REACTIONS

Look back through your daily journal entries and Analyze Ourbursts worksheets so far and list the triggers you've noticed on this chart. Once you have listed the initial reactions/behaviors and what triggers each, talk to your child about working together to change the behaviors:

1. Ask your child what happened to cause their inappropriate reaction.

2. Ask your child to name appropriate alternative behaviors. It's okay to lead them to ideas if they can't come up with any on their own, but this should be a team effort if you need to help.

3. Ask your child if their recent inappropriate reaction is on that list of appropriate behaviors.

4. Reiterate that the next time that trigger occurs, they should do one of the things on the appropriate reactions list.

Stick with it! Behavior modification is tough and takes a lot of time.

EVENT: CHILD'S INITIAL REACTION, i.e., OUTBURST OR MELTDOWN

⬇

WHAT TRIGGERED THIS REACTION?

⬇

SAY TO MY CHILD...

What was unacceptable about _____ ?

What happened to cause you to _____ ?

Please tell me some different reactions that would be more appropriate.

⬇

APPROPRIATE ALTERNATIVE BEHAVIORS/REACTIONS *(identified by your child)*

⬇

STRATEGIES FOR PREFERRED OUTCOMES
(What can you do to help your child in this situation in the future?)

RELINQUISH CONTROL

You must teach your child independence by giving them some control to facilitate a happier household. List below some times when you could let your child with ADHD make the decisions, by either giving them a couple of acceptable choices to select from, or letting them make a decision without any ~~hovering~~ guidance. Come back and add more items to this list as they become apparent, or as your child gets older and can handle more responsibility.

>> _____

>> _____

>> _____

>> _____

>> _____

>> _____

>> _____

>> _____

>> _____

Step 6: Implement the Plan

》》》》》**》**》》》

"A good idea is about ten percent. Implementation, hard work, and luck is 90 percent."

— Guy Kawasaki

Lift Them Up

Before you can help your child and your family reach a better place living with ADHD, you have to rebuild your child's foundation. Children with ADHD usually have low self-esteem — they are very aware that they can't always keep up with their peers in the classroom and/or on the playground. It is defeating to see your holiday poem on the bulletin board outside your fourth grade classroom look more like the poems posted in the kindergarten hall. It's tough to have your classroom behavior card turned to yellow or orange every day. Each of these things chips away a bit at a time and compounds to create very low self-esteem and a faulty foundation.

As you implement your plan to improve your child's behavior and ADHD symptoms, be sure to include the following ideas to rebuild their self-esteem and self-confidence:

> Remain positive by focusing on your child's strengths more than their weaknesses.

> Explain ADHD to your child so they know they have a difference in the way they were made, and reiterate that they are not stupid or lazy. Be honest with them about the disorder, but still remain optimistic in your description.

> Praise them monumentally for their accomplishments *every single day*.

> Help them discover activities they are interested in and/or good at, and offer opportunities to nurture those interests. (We'll talk about this more in *Step 9: Enjoy Your Child*.)

> Make them feel special in every way you can.

Behavior Modification

Rome wasn't built in a day. You can't change your child's undesirable behaviors all at once. This is a marathon not a sprint. Get it? I know it's hard not to work on everything at once, because we are parents and we want to "fix" things. But this thing, ADHD, can't be fixed at all, and its behaviors can't be modified in a single day, week, or month even. An ADHD brain is fast and chaotic, so parents must repeat lessons and keep everything simple to be effective.

Make a List

Start by making a list of all the behaviors you'd like to work on. Then reorder the list by priority with the #1 behavior you'd like to tackle at the top. I recommend you start with risky or unsafe behaviors first. Then move on to the behaviors that happen most frequently. This is your behavior modification to-do list for your child. I acknowledge that this sounds like you are trying to change your child's essence and that feels wrong. Teaching children to think before they act and react to social situations appropriately isn't changing them; it's teaching them what should be intrinsic skills, but aren't due to their ADHD. You can call it the Lagging Skills To-Do List if that feels better.

Record Statistics

The best way to measure your child's success and your behavior modification strategy for each individual goal is to frequently track outcomes. For reliable data, take measurements often. Measure success for each current behavioral goal no less than four times a day. Give your child a check mark, a star, or a sticker every time they successfully meet the behavior goal for each increment throughout each day. Leave it blank if they did not meet the goal during that measurement period; do not put an X or any mark there if the goal was not met. You are rewarding and praising the good progress and ignoring no progress. This is effective, I promise — it's effective without detriment to their self-esteem. The visual nature of a chart helps your child see when they are doing well or when they need to work harder to improve, and it helps you measure the effectiveness of your plan at a quick glance.

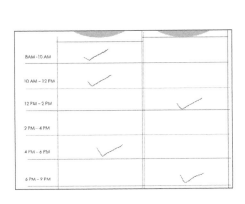 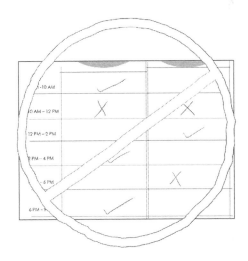

Your child should progress to meet the goal more often each day. However, regressions in behavior are common with ADHD, so don't let one or two bad days throw you off or lead you to quit. Be consistent and keep working at it long-term.

Once your child is meeting their behavior goal almost every time it's measured and consistently for at least two to four weeks, it's time to begin working on their next behavioral/skills goal. Repeat these steps with each and every goal one at a time. If you and your child can handle it, you can work on two goals at once after mastering the first, but never more than two goals at a time. Behavior modification becomes less effective the more goals you target at once, in my experience. Ricochet has only been able to handle two goals at a time with success.

Reward Progress

Human beings are more likely to work harder if they are recognized for their accomplishments — praise and rewards can motivate anyone. You often earn greater results when acknowledging the accomplishments of a child with ADHD because they are used to getting more negative feedback than positive, unfortunately.

> *Reward and praise the good progress and ignore no progress.*

Rewards, including praise, need to be presented more often for children with ADHD. They tend to live in the moment, so they need frequent feedback to stay on track. Rewards don't have to be tangible items like toys or money — they can be social rewards like praise or a sleep-over with a friend. I recommend a mix of the two because your child needs to hear you say great things about them, and you can't get a tangible prize every time you make the right choice in life anyway.

Behavior modification is a long-term undertaking but necessary to prepare your child with ADHD for life in the real world. You can't facilitate their choices all their lives, so you have to teach them critical thinking skills before they are grown.

Environmental Modification

There are many things in an individual's environment that can cause over-stimulation and undesirable feelings and/or behavior. However, there are also supportive environments for kids with ADHD, too. As logic dictates, you want to minimize the negative environmental factors and maximize the time spent in more supportive environments.

Negative Environmental Factors

Anything that causes over-stimulation for your child should be reduced or eliminated in their environment — for instance, bright lights, fluorescent lights, loud sounds or a noisy setting, strong odors, and cluttered surroundings can all cause over-stimulation. When children become over-stimulated, they are distracted by the sensory stimuli that are bothering them, reducing the ability to focus and often causing their behavior to deteriorate.

Modify your child's environments to reduce over-stimulation as much as possible. Keep interior décor simple and soft, especially in their personal spaces. When you visit other environments that you can't control, such as an event outdoors on a sunny day or a birthday party at a kids' arcade, be prepared to attempt to mitigate over-stimulation or keep your time in that environment brief. An example might be to buy your child sunglasses and put up a tent for shade if bright sunlight overwhelms them. Or, let your child listen to music through headphones while playing games at the arcade to drown out some of the extraneous noise and auditory chaos. There are often ways to mitigate over-stimulation with a little forethought so your special child can participate in most activities without distress.

In addition, when you know you are entering an environment that will be challenging for them, always discuss with your child what they should expect. Give them the option of being in that environment or not. If they choose to go, enlist their help in determining ways to help them cope with undesirable elements. Here's an example of how to approach this:

"I know bright sunshine bothers you, so we are taking your sunglasses and a shade tent to the family picnic today. Is there anything else you can think of that we should take to help you with the bright sun? I know the sunglasses and tent are going to make you more comfortable, but if you still become uneasy, let me know right away and we will work on resolving it together."

Your child should not have to miss activities and events due to environment when you can mitigate many factors that may over-stimulate. Plan ahead and you can make your child's participation comfortable.

Positive Environments

Many environments can be calming or soothing to children with ADHD, too. According to recent studies, kids with ADHD who routinely play in green outdoor settings, such as a grassy open field or a park, experience milder ADHD symptoms. That's part of the reason outdoor play is so often recommended for kids with ADHD[10]. Be sure to find a setting without too much noise or other troublesome stimuli so your child will feel relaxed.

As well, indoor environments illuminated by natural light, with a muted, soothing color on the walls (that does NOT include white), and very simple, minimal décor are great for kids with ADHD. When considering your child's environment, remember that the softer, quieter, and more minimal, the better for a child with ADHD — maybe evaluate the environment through the perspective of a comfortable setting for an infant.

When considering any environment for children with ADHD, whether it's temporary or long-term, consider the following factors *through your child's perspective:*

> ❯ the severity or harshness of the light
> ❯ the softness of the wall color

> ❯ the noise level, including soft, consistent sounds that might annoy such as the buzzing of a light bulb or the hum of a motor

> ❯ the texture of surfaces (hard or soft, rough or smooth, etc.)

> ❯ how open and green outdoor play spaces are

> ❯ the level of visual clutter

> ❯ the amount of structure and predictability provided by the environment

Taking a little time to evaluate your child's environments and make appropriate changes provides the opportunity to reduce oversensitivity and allay a potential increase in ADHD symptoms.

Diet Modification

American grocery stores are plagued with ~~chemistry projects~~ highly-processed foods (obviously, I use the term "food" loosely in this instance). Nutritionists always advise to do your shopping on the outer perimeter of the grocery store — that's where all the fresh foods (produce, meat, and dairy) are displayed. Most of these products are natural, yet the processed foods are filled with ingredients imagined in a laboratory and produced in a factory. And many of those ingredients created in the laboratory can cause neurological side effects, not to mention other health dangers[11].

Color by Number and ADHD

One of the biggest offenders in the grocery aisles for most with ADHD is artificial food coloring, often denoted by the color name and then a number after it (Red #40, Yellow #5, etc.). These are highly-concentrated chemicals plain and simple. The Food and Drug Administration (FDA) allows them in food production in the U.S., but they have been banned in several other countries due to their potentially harmful side effects[12].

Studies have shown that Red #40 can cause aggression and impulsivity in many children, and Yellow #5 is often associated with hyperactivity and negative behavioral reactions in children[13]. Look for natural colorants on labels — beets, turmeric, or carrots — when you have to buy packaged foods.

I know first-hand the massive effect Red #40 can have on a child who is sensitive to it — Ricochet becomes an aggressive, moody monster for hours after drinking a red Gatorade. He drank his last a few years ago when we finally made the correlation. He can occasionally have an item that contains a tiny amount of Red #40 in it, but nothing with colossal amounts like red beverages. He might as well pick up a beaker in a high school chemistry lab and drink it. Ricochet after red Gatorade is just like that, as though he drank an experimental potion in a lab — he turns from Dr. Jekyll into unpredictable and violent Mr. Hyde.

I get very worked up about artificial colors. There is simply no need to use them in food production. Many U.S. companies are successfully manufacturing the same products with natural colorants overseas in countries that have banned artificial colors. We know some people can't tolerate them — research studies have scientifically proven that — and yet the majority of processed foods contain them. My favorite example of this ludicrousness is marshmallows — they contain blue and yellow artificial coloring, yet the product is *white*. Why not offer a red-flavored Gatorade with cherry or pomegranate to color it? Or, just tell me the flavor of a clear drink for goodness sake; Americans are smarter than big business gives us credit for. {Sheesh!} While the FDA won't protect us, avoid artificial colors and protect yourselves and your families.

Other Chemicals in Food

There are many chemical ingredients allowed in food production by the FDA, not just artificial colors. There are artificial flavors, artificial sweeteners, chemical preservatives, wax on produce, etc. — all of which can have a negative effect on the neurological system and cause undesirable behaviors[14]. Of course, there are pesticides on our produce too[15], only avoided by eating entirely certified-organic foods. That proposition is enormously expensive, but, if you have the means to do it, you definitely should. I wish my family could!

I strongly advise you to stay away from artificial dyes and other chemical ingredients to the fullest extent possible. It's a healthy decision for your entire family, but is essential for your child with ADHD. No one told me about the potentially harmful effects of artificial ingredients in food, not even when my son was diagnosed with ADHD. It was well over a year after his diagnosis before I ran across the astonishing correlation in my research. Ricochet had one red Gatorade after that, and then I knew his aggression immediately after drinking it was due to the devious Red #40 the U.S. government deems innocuous.

Protein Is Your New BFF

A high-protein diet, especially for breakfast, is wise for most individuals, but particularly for those with ADHD. Protein from your diet is used to make neurotransmitters, the chemical messengers of the brain. It also reduces blood-sugar spikes that can cause hyperactivity. In total, a high-protein meal promotes attention and alertness.

Complex carbohydrates, like vegetables and some fruits, are a recommended complement to protein-rich foods. Avoid simple carbohydrates — white bread, white rice, potatoes, etc. — as they are either loaded with sugar or are converted to sugar during digestion. Complex carbohydrates with protein-rich foods will keep one satisfied longer and the body at optimal performance.

Some protein-rich foods ideal for the breakfast plates of kids with ADHD include:

> eggs, just about any way you want to prepare them — add cheese or meat to pack a bigger protein punch

> nut spreads on whole grain toast, fruit, or celery

> yogurt, especially Greek yogurt

> protein shakes, homemade is best, or buy premade supplement shakes like Boost or Ensure

> mixed nuts or trail mix

> protein bars (just steer clear of those with lots of sugar and artificial ingredients)

> breakfast protein cookies (www.trasnfitblog.com has a great recipe at http://bit.ly/BreakfastProteinCookie)

> waffles or pancakes made with coconut, oat, or almond flour (**NOT** white flour)

> cottage cheese

IMPLEMENT BEHAVIOR MODIFICATION

Make a list of behaviors your child with ADHD exhibits that you'd like to change (the triggers chart is a good source of troubling behaviors). Be realistic. After you create the list of behaviors to tackle on the left, prioritize them to the right. Then, write the first two behavior goals you'd like to start working on at the bottom.

1 BEHAVIORS TO WORK ON ARE:

-
-
-
-
-
-
-
-
-
-
-

2 NOW PRIORITIZE THEM TO ESTABLISH THE ORDER YOU'LL TACKLE THEM IN:

1.
2.
3.
4.
5.
6.
7.
8.
9.
10.

Start behavior modification here

3 THE TWO BEHAVIORS I WANT TO TACKLE FIRST ARE:

1. _____

2. _____

GOALS CHART

Use this chart to measure and track your child's progress toward their behavior goals. Set the rewards based on your individual child and what motivates them to work hard toward their goal. The first chart is a sample.

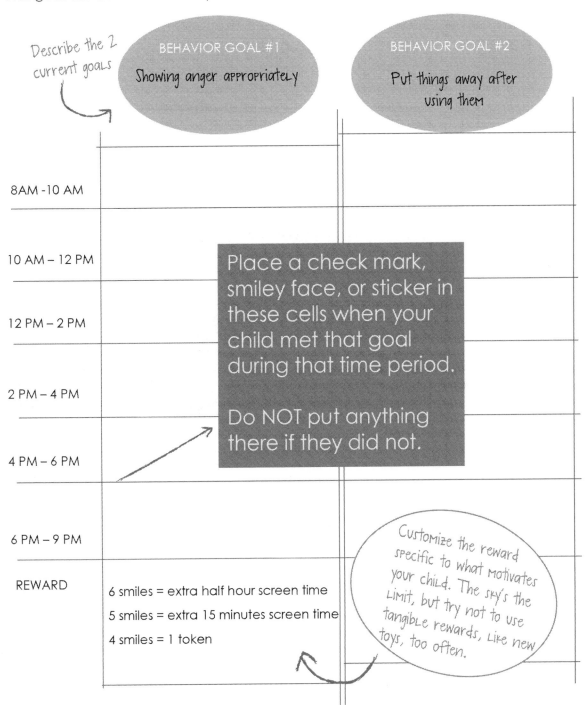

Describe the 2 current goals

BEHAVIOR GOAL #1
Showing anger appropriately

BEHAVIOR GOAL #2
Put things away after using them

8AM - 10 AM		
10 AM – 12 PM		
12 PM – 2 PM		
2 PM – 4 PM		
4 PM – 6 PM		
6 PM – 9 PM		
REWARD	6 smiles = extra half hour screen time 5 smiles = extra 15 minutes screen time 4 smiles = 1 token	

Place a check mark, smiley face, or sticker in these cells when your child met that goal during that time period.

Do NOT put anything there if they did not.

Customize the reward specific to what motivates your child. The sky's the limit, but try not to use tangible rewards, like new toys, too often.

GOALS CHART

Use this chart to measure and track your child's progress toward their behavior goals. Set the rewards based on your individual child and what motivates them to work hard toward their goal.

Describe the 2
current goals

	BEHAVIOR GOAL #1	BEHAVIOR GOAL #2
8AM -10 AM		
10 AM – 12 PM		
12 PM – 2 PM		
2 PM – 4 PM		
4 PM – 6 PM		
6 PM – 9 PM		
REWARD		

POWER BREAKFAST

High protein is so important to start the day for kids with ADHD. This is the kind of energy that can be sustained and help mental cognition. Use this weekly chart to plan your breakfast menu to ensure you always feed your child a protein-rich breakfast.

MON / /

TUES / /

WED / /

THURS / /

FRI / /

SAT / /

SUN / /

Some ideas of protein-rich foods for breakfast include:

Protein shake

Whole wheat toast with nut butter

Eggs (add cheese for bigger protein boost)

Protein drinks like Ensure or Boost

Meat (can be anything, not just sausage or bacon)

Cheese stick/string cheese

Greek yogurt

Tofu

Beef or turkey jerky

Ants on a log (peanut butter and raisins on celery)

Protein bars

Whole wheat pita and hummus

Cottage cheese

Kefir

Soy beans

Nut bars (such as Kind bars)

Sunflower or pumpkin seeds

Whole wheat bagel with cream cheese

Protein breakfast cookies

Step 7: Get a Handle on ADHD at School

"You can't eat straight A's."
—Maxine Hong Kingston

School. {Argh!} I don't even want to think about it long enough to write this section, but I will trudge on in the hopes of helping you avoid some of the same devastation we've slogged through over the last several years.

Every Individual with ADHD is Just that, an Individual.

No two people are alike. While many disorders and diseases present with the same symptoms or tell-tale signs for everyone, that is not the case for ADHD. It can manifest to varying degrees and through different symptoms and behaviors. What works for Mary's child may not work for your child. This is an especially important fact to remember when working with your child's school, in order to ensure they implement appropriate accommodations and services for the individual constellation of your child's needs, so your child has the opportunity to achieve academic success.

There is no formula to educate a child with ADHD, especially when you layer in other conditions that commonly occur with ADHD. My son has ADHD, but also sensory processing disorder (SPD), anxiety, dysgraphia, written expression disorder, significant executive functioning (EF) delays, and a gifted IQ. That is a very distinctive set of needs, and his education must be tailored accordingly. Your child with ADHD is completely different from mine — your child's education must also be crafted according to their individual needs. It doesn't matter what works for my child because his accommodations may not be pertinent to your child's *individual* needs. Follow these steps to advocate for your child's special needs in their educational environment and open the door to potential academic success.

Advocate, Advocate, Advocate!

No one is going to fight for the success and happiness of a child like their parent will. You are your child's champion and their #1 advocate. When you think they are being treated inappropriately or unfairly, especially considering their ADHD (a disability), you must speak up and fight for them. They have a legal right to the same educational opportunities their neuro-typical peers are offered. That's correct; your child has the *legal right* to a Free Appropriate Public Education (FAPE), which essentially means a legal guarantee of access to an education, whatever that looks like *for them*.

School is the most problematic part of parenting my child with ADHD, as it is for many families in similar circumstances. Ricochet has learning disabilities in addition to his ADHD, so the school environment is often like a round hole for my square-peg kid. I could tell dozens of harrowing stories about our experiences with school, both public and private, but you can read our tale in detail in my previous book, *Boy Without Instructions: Surviving the Learning Curve of Parenting a Child with ADHD.*

There are many parents who want to protect their children from the scrutiny of public opinion and decide to guard their child's ADHD diagnosis as a closely-held, scandalous family secret. Frankly, I don't understand this. In addition to perpetuating the very stigmas that parents are seeking to protect their children from, secrecy breeds shame. This is magnified significantly to children with disorders, such as ADHD, that permeate their sense of self-esteem. Why would you send your child into school under circumstances you know will cause him to struggle and feel bad about himself? That's knowingly setting your child up for failure. If you scrutinize that rationality, you are intentionally allowing your child harm.

If your child needed eyeglasses to be able to complete their worksheets at school, you wouldn't think twice about having their eyes tested and getting them eyeglasses. The glasses bring everything into focus. Some kids may call him "four-eyes," but you'd furnish some whippy comebacks and encourage him to ignore the naysayers. You'd provide what he needs to bring his school work into focus and be successful, and then prepare him for answering to potential bullying.

Why is it not the same for ADHD? Medication and accommodations are tools to sharpen focus as well, in school and in all areas of life. Sure, I completely agree that giving your child stimulant medication is different than furnishing eyeglasses. But the benefit of that and classroom accommodations, the increased focus, can give your child the opportunity to achieve success. Well, when you put it like that…

Alright. Jumping off my soapbox now.

Talk with your child's teachers and make sure they understand his weaknesses, and his strengths, too. If someone can help, why would you not want them to? Keeping your child's disability a secret negatively impacts the advocacy process. The most valuable source of information on how your child's disability impacts them at school is *your child*. There are school personnel who will say to parents, "We could classify your child for special education, but do you really want them to be labeled that way?" That is an unfair statement that exploits the fears many parents have about social stigmas and directly prevents children from getting the services they need. On the other hand, speaking to your child openly and having them drive this process is incredibly empowering to them, gives you specific information on how their disability impacts their learning, and, most importantly, begins the process of teaching them to advocate for themselves when they go on to college, where they will be required to self-report their disability and request accommodations in order to be protected under the law. (See upcoming section on *Child Find and RTI*.) Our school struggles started before Ricochet was diagnosed with ADHD. In fact, they started on the very first day of kindergarten. His kindergarten teacher insinuated Mr. T and I hadn't prepared him for school or hadn't given him enough independent responsibility at home to encourage success at school. She never recommended we have him evaluated for learning disabilities — not one time!

Uh, NO! This is a school environment issue and, therefore, a learning problem.

Ricochet was diagnosed with ADHD in November of his first grade year, after a different teacher and a different school didn't resolve his classroom issues. The only thing our diagnosing doctor suggested regarding school was to ask for a 504 Plan and then cross my fingers and hope the school complied with the request. He even told me I was wasting my time when I appealed the decision to deny Ricochet special education and an Individualized Educational Plan (IEP) when he was first evaluated by the school in first grade. In fact, he told me Ricochet didn't qualify for an IEP — and that's part of the reason we have been seeing a different ADHD doctor for the last four years. I knew there was more to Ricochet's story than just ADHD. I knew he needed the level of intervention only offered under an IEP (and we got it two years later).

So I trudged along in the muck of managing ADHD and school on my own and without any information, much less a how-to guide on securing appropriate services at school for a special needs child. I felt like a tiny old lady jogging onto the football field, never having seen a game of football much less played one, and no one advised me to wear protective gear. Like a knight entering a sword fight with a Nerf sword and no armor and no strategy. I was completely ignorant about the system I was trying to break into and left to figure it out on my own. To this day, I'm still trying to figure out its intricacies, and I'm always pushing back against a system designed to do as little as possible rather than strive for excellence for all children.

Your Child Has Rights

In the eyes of *"the law,"* ADHD is officially a disability. As a disability it entitles your child to special services and accommodations within the public school system, spelled out in only minor detail under the Individuals with Disabilities Education Improvement Act (IDEA) and Section 504 of the Rehabilitation Act of 1973 (Section 504). Yes, your child has a right to assistance in school on one level or another if his ADHD negatively affects his life skill of learning. And there's no reason not to take advantage of it.

However, and this is a big HOWEVER, most school administrators encourage their staff to reject a child for special services if at all possible. It's shocking that a child's needs aren't first priority at school of all places, but that is a decision often driven by dreadful school budgets and bureaucracy. On the contrary though, the law says a child's IEP must be drafted without any influence of financial limitations. Highlight this paragraph and dog-ear this page as there's great potential you'll have to reference this portion of the IDEA code for school administrators at some point in your child's school career, maybe many times.

I will point out some key phrases throughout this section that are very useful to include in your arguments when ~~pleading with~~ encouraging the school to provide the services or accommodations your child needs. Watch for these key words and phrases in sidebars within this chapter.

Let's dive in by starting at the beginning...

What is Section 504?

Section 504 of the Rehabilitation Act of 1973 is a federal law that protects qualified individuals — those with disabilities — from discrimination based on their disability. It requires that the educational needs of students with disabilities are served as adequately as non-disabled students. Section 504 protects those with a physical or mental impairment that substantially limits one or more major life activities — the "life activity"

> *The best way to understand how your child's disability is impacting their experience at school is to openly discuss it with them.*

that concerns us in relation to a student with ADHD at school is learning. All schools and all school districts must acknowledge Section 504 protections; participation is not optional.

It is important to note that the standard under Section 504, which is similar to that in IDEA, is that the disability must "substantially impact a major life activity." A diagnosis of ADHD, or any other disability in and of itself, does not entitle a student to anything. Parents must show how the child's major life activity (i.e., learning) is impacted. The best way to understand how your child's disability is impacting their experience at school is to openly discuss it with them.

A 504 Plan for educational purposes is usually drafted and maintained by a committee within the school or school district. More often than not, the parent must request a 504 Plan for their child; schools don't usually approach a parent and offer legal protections for students. If you wish to request a 504 Plan for your child, submit your request in writing to the principal and get confirmation of receipt (there's a sample letter at the end of this chapter).

The 504 Plan will state the disability and the life activity that the disability limits for that student. Then the committee, which almost always includes the student's classroom teacher, will decide on and list appropriate accommodations the student needs implemented to gain equivalent opportunities to their non-disabled peers for academic success. Parents don't have a right by law to participate in the formation of their child's 504 Plan, but you should always request to participate; you know your child best.

Academic Success

is a great buzz phrase to use when communicating with the school about your child's special needs in the educational environment. As a child with a disability, your child has a legal right to accommodations that will even the playing field with their non-disabled peers to provide the same opportunity for academic success. While the school doesn't always define "academic success" in the same way parents do, it is the ultimate goal under the law.

Following is a list of possible accommodations for a student with ADHD — this list is only a sample of the limitless possibilities, as the 504 Plan must be individualized for each qualifying student.

> › extra time to complete assignments and tests

> permission to utilize fidgets in the classroom

> the ability to move around when peers are required to sit still in their chairs

> the opportunity to retreat to a quieter location when necessary

> permission to chew gum

> teacher records homework assignments for student daily

> teacher maintains supplies

> preferential seating

> sensory breaks

> modified assignments

> daily parent-teacher communication

> etc...

Free Appropriate Public Education

Also often referred to as FAPE, this is a phrase you need to add to your vocabulary as a parent of a child with ADHD. This is your child's right under federal law as a child with a disability. It is often effective to include this exact phrase in conversations and written communications about accommodations and special services within the school. Be sure not to use phrases like "maximize my child's potential" though, as that is not their right under the law. Use "level the playing field to achieve FAPE" instead.

This is an example of showing the flexibility of accommodations under 504 and underscores the importance of speaking to your child. The best way to know what accommodations to ask for is to ask your child what the most difficult thing about school is and how you can help.

What is IDEA?

IDEA is an acronym, short for the Individuals with Disabilities Education Improvement Act. The law was enacted in 1975 to ensure that children with disabilities have the opportunity to receive a Free Appropriate Public Education, the same as non-disabled children. This is a U.S. federal law that defines the educational rights of individuals with disabilities. It is important to note that ADHD alone doesn't automatically qualify a child for inclusion in the special education program or for an Individualized Education Plan (IEP). IDEA provides more services and interventions than a 504 Plan, and provides a rigid procedural structure with added administrative oversight by the Commissioner of the Department of Education.

While the overarching right for students under IDEA is a Free and Appropriate Public Education, the law lists several additional rights for students and their parents:

1. Free Appropriate Public Education: an education suited to the needs of the child with a disability; in my opinion, it also means that the student with a disability gets equal access to academic success.

2. Appropriate Evaluation: Evaluators must be knowledgeable and trained, and must use a variety of tools to gather information about the student.

3. Individualized Educational Plan (IEP): a written education plan tailored to that student's needs that is developed, maintained, and reviewed according to the law.

4. Least Restrictive Environment: It is assumed that students with disabilities are best educated among their non-disabled peers unless the nature of their disability prevents successful learning in the regular education classroom. The Least Restrictive Environment (LRE) is the environment that is best for your child's learning and success and as close to a regular education classroom as possible. In fact, many schools are required to provide "push-in" services (where a special education teacher comes into the regular education classroom to provide services) as opposed to "pull-out" services (where the student leaves the regular

education classroom to go to the special education classroom for individual or group services) whenever feasible.

5. Parent and Student Participation: Parents have the right to participate in all decision-making regarding school placement and drafting and revision of the IEP. The student has a right to share preferences and participate in designing the IEP as well.

6. Procedural Safeguards: Parents of a child receiving special education services have the right to safeguards like notification, informed consent, copies of all evaluations and records, dispute resolution, and a few others.

So how do you know if your child with ADHD qualifies for special services under IDEA? The definition of "a child with a disability" within IDEA spells out eligibility for services under IDEA. Here's the definition of a child with a disability directly from the law code (author edited to remove portions not applicable to the audience of this book).

§ 300.8 CHILD WITH A DISABILITY.

(A) GENERAL. (1) CHILD WITH A DISABILITY MEANS A CHILD EVALUATED IN ACCORDANCE WITH §§300.304 THROUGH 300.311 AS HAVING INTELLECTUAL DISABILITY**, A HEARING IMPAIRMENT (INCLUDING DEAFNESS), A SPEECH OR LANGUAGE IMPAIRMENT, A VISUAL IMPAIRMENT (INCLUDING BLINDNESS), A SERIOUS EMOTIONAL DISTURBANCE (REFERRED TO IN THIS PART AS "EMOTIONAL DISTURBANCE"), AN ORTHOPEDIC IMPAIRMENT, AUTISM, TRAUMATIC BRAIN INJURY, AN OTHER HEALTH IMPAIRMENT, A SPECIFIC LEARNING DISABILITY, DEAF-BLINDNESS, OR MULTIPLE DISABILITIES, AND WHO, BY REASON THEREOF, NEEDS SPECIAL EDUCATION AND RELATED SERVICES...

(C) DEFINITIONS OF DISABILITY TERMS. THE TERMS USED IN THIS DEFINITION OF A CHILD WITH A DISABILITY ARE DEFINED AS FOLLOWS:...

(4)(I) EMOTIONAL DISTURBANCE MEANS A CONDITION EXHIBITING ONE OR MORE OF THE FOLLOWING CHARACTERISTICS OVER A LONG PERIOD OF TIME AND TO A MARKED DEGREE THAT ADVERSELY AFFECTS A CHILD'S EDUCATIONAL PERFORMANCE:

(A) AN INABILITY TO LEARN THAT CANNOT BE EXPLAINED BY INTELLECTUAL, SENSORY, OR HEALTH FACTORS.

(B) AN INABILITY TO BUILD OR MAINTAIN SATISFACTORY INTERPERSONAL RELATIONSHIPS WITH PEERS AND TEACHERS.

(C) INAPPROPRIATE TYPES OF BEHAVIOR OR FEELINGS UNDER NORMAL CIRCUMSTANCES.

(D) A GENERAL PERVASIVE MOOD OF UNHAPPINESS OR DEPRESSION.

(E) A TENDENCY TO DEVELOP PHYSICAL SYMPTOMS OR FEARS ASSOCIATED WITH PERSONAL OR SCHOOL PROBLEMS.

(II) EMOTIONAL DISTURBANCE INCLUDES SCHIZOPHRENIA. THE TERM DOES NOT APPLY TO CHILDREN WHO ARE SOCIALLY MALADJUSTED, UNLESS IT IS DETERMINED THAT THEY HAVE AN EMOTIONAL DISTURBANCE UNDER PARAGRAPH (C)(4)(I) OF THIS SECTION...

*(6) INTELLECTUAL DISABILITY ** MEANS SIGNIFICANTLY SUBAVERAGE GENERAL INTELLECTUAL FUNCTIONING, EXISTING CONCURRENTLY WITH DEFICITS IN ADAPTIVE BEHAVIOR AND MANIFESTED DURING THE DEVELOPMENTAL PERIOD, THAT ADVERSELY AFFECTS A CHILD'S EDUCATIONAL PERFORMANCE...*

(9) OTHER HEALTH IMPAIRMENT MEANS HAVING LIMITED STRENGTH, VITALITY, OR ALERTNESS, INCLUDING A HEIGHTENED ALERTNESS TO ENVIRONMENTAL STIMULI, THAT RESULTS IN LIMITED ALERTNESS WITH RESPECT TO THE EDUCATIONAL ENVIRONMENT, THAT—

(I) IS DUE TO CHRONIC OR ACUTE HEALTH PROBLEMS SUCH AS ASTHMA, ATTENTION DEFICIT DISORDER OR ATTENTION DEFICIT HYPERACTIVITY DISORDER, DIABETES, EPILEPSY, A HEART CONDITION, HEMOPHILIA, LEAD POISONING, LEUKEMIA, NEPHRITIS, RHEUMATIC FEVER, SICKLE CELL ANEMIA, AND TOURETTE SYNDROME; AND

(II) ADVERSELY AFFECTS A CHILD'S EDUCATIONAL PERFORMANCE[16].

"Academic Performance" is More than Just Grades

There are many ways for parents to establish need when their child's academic performance does not necessarily show that they are failing. Each school year, parents receive a code of conduct from the school. If parents read through this document, they would be shocked at how many things the school reserves the right to use to evaluate their children that have nothing to do with academics. They are required to be prompt, respectful, organized, well-groomed, respect the property of others, and on and on. In addition to that, a full column of your child's report card is dedicated to evaluating them for non-academic criteria. Think about the column that contains comments such as "disrespectful," "talks out in class," "tests well, but is disruptive," "highly disorganized," "tests well, but doesn't turn in assignments on time or at all." These are methods that the school district uses to evaluate your children regardless of whether they are passing or failing. Point these things out when seeking services or accommodations.

Robert M. Tudisco, Attorney, Non-Profit Consultant, and Motivational Speaker

As you can see, ADHD is referenced under the eligibility standard of "Other Health Impaired." Just because ADHD is listed in the law doesn't mean your child with ADHD is automatically eligible for special education services though, believe me. The law further quantifies it as "chronic" and **it must "adversely affect the child's educational performance."** If your child is doing well in school, they don't qualify for, nor do they need special services and an IEP for ADHD. "Doing well in school" does not mean straight A's either — it's more than just grades. Parents are often told their children are not entitled to classification or accommodations because they are not failing. IDEA regulation 300.10 specifically addresses this issue, requiring the school to provide special education services to a disabled child even though the child has not failed or been retained in a course or grade and is advancing from grade to grade. (Highlight that! Your IEP team will stand up and take notice for sure if you start quoting regulation numbers from IDEA!)

In a letter dated November 2007, The Department of Education's Office of Special Education Programs responded to the lack of definition for the eligibility phrase "adversely affects the child's educational performance" in the IDEA law, stating:

"...Although the phrase 'adversely affects educational performance' is not specifically defined, the extent of the impact that the child's impairment or condition has on the child's educational performance is a decisive factor in a child's eligibility determination under Part B [of IDEA]. We believe that the evaluation and eligibility determination processes... are sufficient for the group of qualified professionals and the parent to ascertain how the child's impairment or disability affects the child's ability to function in an educational setting. A range of factors — both academic and nonacademic — can be considered in making this determination for each individual child. See 34 CFR §300.306(c). Even if a child is advancing from grade to grade or is placed in the regular educational environment for most or all of the school day, the group charged with making the eligibility determination still could determine that the child's impairment or condition adversely affects the child's educational performance because the child could not progress satisfactorily in the absence of specific instructional adaptations or supportive services, including modifications to the general education curriculum. 34 CFR §300.101(c) (regarding requirements for individual eligibility determinations for children advancing from grade to grade).

Based on section 607(e) of the IDEA, we are informing you that our response is provided as informal guidance and is not legally binding, but represents an interpretation by the U.S. Department of Education of the IDEA in the context of the specific facts presented[17].

In other words, it's up to the group of qualified professionals (i.e., your child's IEP team) and the participating parent to decide if the child's disability "adversely affects the child's educational performance." This determination has been a source of contention for many an IEP team and parent, and will be for years to come. You are essentially at the mercy of the school personnel's interpretation of the law on this matter (and their special services budget), then you can file for a hearing if you disagree.

A significant difference between Section 504 and IDEA is that IDEA requires a child to be classified for special education, while 504 does not. Historically, IDEA did not include ADHD as a classifiable disorder. It was not until the 1997 reauthorization of IDEA that ADHD was added to the Other Health Impaired (OHI) category, after much lobbying by parent organizations like the non-profit, CHADD (Children and Adults with Attention Deficit Hyperactivity Disorder). There are many school districts in the U.S. whose policy is a leftover from the pre-1997 addition of ADHD to IDEA. Before then, all children diagnosed with ADHD were given 504 plans. Many school districts tell parents that students with ADHD are not entitled to services under IDEA because students with ADHD get 504 plans. *That is not the law!* That is school district policy, and parents can and should challenge that if they believe their child needs an Individualized Education Plan (IEP) under IDEA.

Evaluation Process

If you think your child with ADHD will qualify for special education services and an IEP based on the eligibility criteria outlined above, your first step is to request an evaluation in writing. The request for evaluation is a letter from the parent(s) to the child's principal stating that you feel your child is struggling to reach academic success and you would like them to be evaluated for learning difficulties (there's a sample letter at the end of this chapter). Most advocates and education attorneys suggest you mail this letter to the principal with a delivery signature required. I emailed this letter to our school principal with delivery receipt and read receipt requested instead, to expedite the process. Once your request is received, the process will begin, *if the school agrees that your child may have a disability.* If the school refuses any request you've made in writing, you can contest their decision by filing for an impartial hearing.

Once the school agrees to the evaluation by asking your permission and receiving your written consent on a special form, the clock starts ticking under the law — that's why it's a good idea to collect confirmation of receipt and an associated date. Once you sign the consent form, the school has sixty days to perform the testing and prepare an eligibility decision.

Child Find and RTI

For K-12 children, both IDEA and Section 504 share a component called "Child Find." This means the school district where the child resides has an obligation to identify children in their school district with special needs, identify those needs, and provide appropriate services. This is true whether the child attends the local public school or not. This is how children attending private schools, or children too young to attend public school, can qualify for services. Keep this in mind when disagreements with the school district arise and when deciding whether or not to request an impartial hearing.

As an attempt to ensure that there is no delay in providing services to young children at crucial developmental stages, the 2004 amendment to IDEA included Response to Intervention (RTI), which gives school districts the ability to provide remedial services in areas such as speech, language, and reading without having to go through the evaluation and IEP process.

In theory, the concept of RTI expedites services without lengthy evaluations, meetings, and IEPs. However, many districts use RTI as a way to circumvent the IEP process. The regulations under IDEA specifically prohibit this, but it happens anyway. While 34 C.F.R Section 300.309(a)(2)(i) allows for information gained from RTI to be included in the evaluation, it is not required under the law. In many cases, parents are stalled by being told that the school is already doing something and that it is too early to evaluate until they know that RTI is not working. *This is not the law* and parents should push back here. In fact, because of this issue, the Department of Education issued a memorandum to each state Department of Education recognizing that "in some instances, local educational agencies (LEA's) may be using Response to Intervention strategies to delay or deny a timely initial evaluation for children suspected of having a disability." It went on to stress that "the use of RTI strategies cannot be used to delay or deny the provision of a full and individual evaluation… to a child suspected of having a disability[18]."

Even in cases where RTI is being utilized and seems to be working, but there are also other issues impacting the student's development, parents should insist on an evaluation to determine what, if any, specific deficits exist and how they should be addressed. There is no reason to delay an evaluation because a child is receiving services through RTI.

Transition and Post-Secondary Education

One thing that IDEA and Section 504 have in common is the concept of "Child Find." For students in K-12, school districts have an affirmative obligation to identify, locate, and evaluate students who they suspect may have a disability, and provide services, support and/or accommodations to provide them with a Free Appropriate Public Education. (20 U.S.C Section 1412(a)(3). But these requirements only apply to students before they graduate from high school.

IDEA only applies to students up to the age of 21 or high school graduation, whichever comes first. In light of this, IDEA requires that the school district develop a transition plan for students between the ages of 14 and 16 who have an IEP. The transition plan addresses whether college, junior college, or vocational training will be most appropriate, how the current services under that student's IEP will translate into accommodations under Section 504 after graduation, and what testing accommodations will be necessary for placement testing such as the SAT or ACT. The transition meeting is important and should definitely include the student.

While Section 504 continues on to post-secondary education, the Child Find component of it ends after high school graduation. What this means is that when your children go off to college, the school has no legal responsibility, unless and until the student self-reports their diagnosis, documents it, and requests reasonable accommodations. If they don't, they have little or no recourse if they fail, even if it is due to their disability. Additionally, under the Family Education Rights and Privacy Act (FERPA), adult students have the exclusive right to their own academic and disciplinary information at school, to the exclusion of everyone else — *even their parents, who are likely paying the tuition.*

The bottom line is that due to the limitations of IDEA, Section 504, and the restrictions under FERPA, post-secondary students MU.S.T be willing to self-report and document their disability in addition to understanding it well enough to articulate their own needs and advocate for themselves. For this reason, including your children in the advocacy process and encouraging them to advocate for themselves at an early age is crucial for their continued success when they get older.

School Testing

The National Dissemination Center for Children with Disabilities (NICHCY), the nation's central source of information on disabilities, offers this overview of the evaluation process: "Evaluating your child means more than the school just giving your child a test. The school must evaluate your child in all the areas where your child may be affected by the possible disability. This may include looking at your child's health, vision, hearing, social and emotional well-being, general intelligence, performance in school, and how well your child communicates with others and uses his or her body. The evaluation must be individualized (just for your child) and full and comprehensive enough to determine if your child has a disability and to identify all of your child's needs for special education and related services if it is determined that your child has a disability[19]."

A school evaluation typically consists of three parts:

1. gathering existing information from teachers, including samples of the student's classroom work;

2. gathering applicable medical records and reporting (with written parent consent for release); and

3. testing for disabilities through written achievement and intelligence testing, other skill-specific industry-standard tests, evaluation by a school psychologist, and more.

It is important to note that most school districts prohibit school personnel from suggesting a diagnosis such as ADHD or autism; they can't evaluate for those medical diagnoses, although they can evaluate behavior at school in regard to its impact on school performance. You must have a private evaluation to receive a *diagnosis* for ADHD. If you suspect ADHD, but don't yet have a formal diagnosis, I recommend that you work on getting the diagnosis privately during the school's evaluation period. You want the school to consider this diagnosis when determining your child's eligibility for special education services. If you already have a diagnosis, provide a copy of that report from your child's physician with the letter to request evaluation.

Could it be more than ADHD?

The National Institute of Mental Health estimates that at least 25 percent of children with ADHD also have a communication/learning disability[20] — my son has two, dysgraphia and written expression disorder. The evaluation for eligibility for special education services will test for specific learning disabilities based on what the committee identifies as possibilities. If you suspect a learning disability, ask that the school test for that learning disability during their evaluation; a specific learning disability seems to virtually guarantee services with or without ADHD.

As well, many children with ADHD also have oppositional defiant disorder (ODD) (50 percent), conduct disorders (40 percent), and anxiety and depression (25 percent)[20]. Given these statistics, it's crucial to also watch for symptoms of these disorders in your children with ADHD. I feel you should share information about these co-existing mental health conditions with your child's school and teachers when necessary, but not otherwise — it's necessary when these conditions affect your child's behavior and/or performance at school. Ricochet has a lot of school-related anxiety; I share that with his teachers so they can help him through stressful situations before his anxiety leads to an outburst.

My Experience

I have endured the evaluation process with my son through the school twice and privately on three separate occasions. The first evaluation began in the fall of

Getting the 504 or IEP is Only Half the Battle

Most advocacy focuses on the first half of the challenge facing parents, which is in getting the services or accommodations they are seeking from the school district. While this requires a specialized approach, it only addresses half the issue. The second half lies in the implementation of that IEP or 504 plan. Parents need to be ever vigilant in following through because several problems can arise, even when you get what you are seeking. For example, regardless of what the IEP or 504 plan says, many times the services or accommodations are not implemented either by the administration or at the classroom level. Other times, even when they are implemented according to your wishes, they may not be effective or appropriate and need to be altered. It is also common to see that what works today needs to be amended based upon your child's progress, or changing developmental needs. It is important here to constantly review what is in the IEP, what your child is getting, and whether it is effective based upon your child's changing needs.

Robert M. Tudisco, Attorney, Non-Profit Consultant, and Motivational Speaker

Ricochet's first grade year based on his classroom teacher's recommendation and my emphatic agreement. They gave him hearing, vision, achievement, and intelligence tests, and he spoke with the school psychologist. I also gave them the physician's report diagnosing ADHD that November, during the later stages of their evaluation process. At that time, in 2008, the criteria for eligibility for special education services in our state was a certain point spread between the score on the achievement test and the score on the intelligence test, and Ricochet's test scores didn't vary enough to qualify. When they broke the bad news to me that day, everyone in the room felt that Ricochet could benefit from special services and an IEP, but their hands were tied at the time. It was enormously frustrating and made me feel completely helpless.

Ricochet was denied special education services that year, but his school set up a 504 Plan with accommodations for ADHD's impact on his learning. I was allowed to participate in that process, and my input was well-valued during our meetings. The 504 Plan was never enough to accommodate for his writing difficulties though.

A couple of months into his third grade year, by then 2010, Ricochet's classroom teacher voiced concern about his writing. In first grade, his writing skills weren't below grade-level enough to suggest a learning disability. By third grade, the gap had widened substantially as his peers' skills had improved and his hadn't; now a learning disability was apparent. His third grade teacher suggested I request another special education evaluation, and I did so the very next day.

The clock started ticking on his 60-day school evaluation in late October that year. I concurrently had him evaluated privately for writing disabilities and executive functioning delays with a psychologist — I wanted to have full ammunition to get him approved for services this time. The private evaluation report specified written expression disorder and significant executive functioning delays. As well, the school had performed some writing-specific tests for evaluation and also concluded he has a specific learning disability in writing.

I breathed a huge sigh of relief and performed a long-overdue happy dance when I heard he had finally been approved for services. My celebration was grossly premature though, as I've learned in the more than three years that have followed since. Approval was only ten percent of the battle — coming to an agreement with the IEP team and receiving full implementation of the IEP day-to-day in the classroom is the real struggle for most parents, and I was no exception. Keeping the IEP and services when your child starts doing well — *because of them* — is also a common battle I am just ~~fighting my way through~~ learning about and experiencing.

The Individualized Education Plan (IEP)

What is it?

The IEP is the document that stipulates your child's tailored educational plan. Every student who receives special education services has an IEP. This document is enforceable under IDEA, but it is not a contract. The IEP must have the following three components:

> **Present Levels of Performance**: The student's strengths and weaknesses are listed here as well as current grades and test scores. Concerns, such as social skills and behavior, should also be included in this section.

> **Annual Goals**: Every IEP must have measurable student goals for that year. These goals will be based on the needs identified in the Present Levels of Performance. The goals should be measured regularly and reported to the parent — most schools are lax with this in my experience, but you should expect to see the actual measurements reported to you. My son's comes in his report card every nine weeks and always says, "making progress toward goal" and "still working toward goal." The law intends it to be more than that. Ask to see the measurements and specific present levels of performance for each IEP goal, as I have also begun to do. This should be communicated in writing by asking for more specifics on how your child's progress is being evaluated and will also help build a paper trail to support you at future meetings or an impartial hearing.

> **Special Education Services:** This section illustrates how the goals will be met. What services does the child need to achieve a Free

Appropriate Public Education while remaining in the least restrictive environment (most often that's the regular education classroom)? Services your child might receive include pull-out small group or one-on-one instruction with a special services teacher, occupational therapy, accommodations and/or modifications, assistive technology, and speech therapy.

How is it created?

A team of educators meets with the parent(s) to write the student's IEP. Attendees must include: a school administrator, the regular classroom teacher(s), the special education teacher, someone who knows and understands the results of the testing, and the parent. That's right, the school cannot exclude your participation in decision-making about your child when it comes to the IEP.

This is a somewhat formal meeting, and it can be quite intimidating for parents. You are walking into a room full of people you likely don't know well to decide your child's educational fate, at least for that year. While there aren't any do-overs per se, parents have the right to request an IEP meeting whenever they feel it's necessary, and modifications can be made at any time with IEP team agreement. In my experience, the school wants to offer as little as possible in the way of services, and parents want all services and accommodations that have any potential to help their child. There's usually an us-against-them overtone from the start, but you should do everything you can to diffuse this, if possible.

Regardless of what the ultimate outcome in the meeting is, it is crucial that you take good notes (or have someone with you that can) and use them to build a record. In the event that the school does not agree with you, put your disagreement in writing in as much detail as possible and file for an impartial

Anatomy of an IEP Meeting

Because of the potential for an adversarial process, it is important for parents to understand the dynamics and psychology of what happens at an IEP meeting, in order to prepare and react productively.

Setting: The law requires that the team meet at least once a year to review the student's short-term and long-term goals and progress toward them. The reality is that each spring, the school has to get through all of the meetings, so the parents are herded like cattle and paraded through the meetings to meet the requirement. The result is that each meeting creates the distinct impression that decisions have been made in advance and parents feel helpless. In order to address this, ask for a meeting at a different time of the year so you have sufficient time to make your case and seek what your child needs without feeling rushed.

Parties: The team is made up of your child's regular education teacher, a special education teacher, the director of special education, the school psychologist and/or evaluator, and in some states, an independent parent member. If you have developed a good relationship with your child's teachers, they will not hurt your position, but due to politics, they are often reluctant to go out on a limb in the meeting. The person who has the least experience in the area of special education and the least experience and information about your child is the Director of Special Education. Unfortunately, that person has the MOST power at the meeting. They are an administrator and are in charge of the special education budget. THAT is who you have to win over. THAT is the person you must convince, by any means necessary, in order to get your child what they need.

Robert M. Tudisco, Attorney, Non-Profit Consultant, and Motivational Speaker due process hearing to challenge their ruling. You are not bound by the decision they make if you disagree.

Our experience with the IEP

Most of the IEP meetings I've attended for Ricochet have been very contentious. I enter meetings with research and ammunition in hand to request the best interventions for my son's academic success. I sit down at a tiny kid table in a tiny kid chair surrounded by three to seven people who all represent the school, but none of whom know my child half as well as I do. The parent is set up to fail in this process right from the start. Now, you can take someone with you to IEP meetings and I strongly advise that, even if it's just a friend who knows nothing about special needs. The moral support of having a friendly face at the table and knowing there is someone there who is on your side is quite valuable.

The first year Ricochet had an IEP, the plan was developed around me as I sat and nodded my head in complete and utter confusion — in fact, the document had already been created before the meeting. I knew there weren't enough goals and accommodations to really help him achieve success in the classroom, but I didn't understand the process enough to affect change during that meeting. I called several subsequent IEP meetings that year, trying to address issues that were still unresolved, but I was met with a lot of opposition. I was told we had to start with the very basic interventions and try each one for a long period of time before rendering it ineffective and moving on to the next. In one meeting, Ricochet's regular education teacher told me, "Ricochet will always have a hard life, and you can't change it — just accept that he will always struggle." I stood up in tears right then and excused myself from the meeting. This momma knows there are strategies to cope with ADHD and improve my son's life. I'd had enough of special education in the public setting already. I enrolled Ricochet in a private school the following year (more on private schools later in this chapter).

The private school did not work out (I now refer to that private school as "School Oh-No"), and Ricochet was back at this same public school after the first quarter of his (first) fourth grade year. I thought things couldn't get worse than the prior year in terms of having to fight tooth and nail for his special education accommodations and services, but boy was I naïve.

Ricochet was placed in a gifted-cluster class with a teacher so bad for kids with special needs that I named her Miss Gulch in my memoir, *Boy Without Instructions: Surviving the Learning Curve of Parenting a Child with ADHD*. This teacher staunchly believed that kids with learning disabilities simply needed to work harder and longer to accomplish the same as their peers. She also thought that gifted students should complete an exponentially larger volume of work, which is ridiculous. Miss Gulch attended IEP meetings and single-handedly ~~held us all hostage~~ caused them to run three to four hours long because she disputed every accommodation, every strategy, and every intervention proposed for Ricochet. It got so bad — after a classroom-clearing meltdown, grades below the norm, quadruple the anxiety he'd had prior, and a Functional Behavioral Analysis meeting where the teacher refused every intervention and I snapped and yelled at her at close range — that the principal moved him to a different teacher's class for the last quarter of that school year. She said she had never moved a student that late in the school year in all her years in administration, and then she promptly retired.

Ricochet had such a bad experience in two different schools that year that we decided it was time to finally hold him back and have him repeat fourth grade. He didn't need retention on an academic basis — he has a gifted IQ and was on or above grade level in all subjects (except writing, where he had a learning disability) — but he was floundering with the social nuances and higher level of accountability expected of fourth grade students, he was scared to death about moving up after that rotten year, and he was just too young to be going into fifth grade in the first place. When I asked to retain him, his special education teacher said that we would "do great emotional harm to him" with that decision. The principal said he was on grade level so he needed to move up. But Mr. T and I knew different — we had asked about retention at the end of every single school year and were always told he'd catch up eventually. Well, he never caught up, and the gap between his capabilities and his peers' was growing ever wider. I finally convinced the principal to write a recommendation for retention when we realized we were moving into a new school district that summer. Ricochet was all for "having a chance to do fourth grade better," as he put it, so he entered fourth grade again at a new school in 2012.

His (second) fourth grade year was an improvement, but not as much as I'd hoped. While the IEP team at the new school always asked for my input and approval in meetings, most of what was added to his IEP was not implemented in the regular education classroom, at least not frequently or consistently. Ricochet still struggled with completing his work, turning in work, and bringing home school communications and his homework, but the environment as a whole was much easier on him. He has just started intermediate school for fifth grade as I write this — I'm anxious about starting over with new teachers, new special education staff, and new administration, but I'm hopeful for what's possible. The physical environment of this brand new school building is amazing — they are all for implementing technology in the classroom, the students switch classes once so they have two teachers for regular education instead of one, and they have more elective-type classes like drama and computer technology. This school environment and his teachers seem much more attuned to his needs so far. We are still early in the honeymoon phase of this new school year though, so I'll have to keep my expectations measured and see how it goes.

I share my personal story on special education and IEPs with you for a few reasons:

1. to illustrate that it is a complicated process for everyone;

2. to share the fact that it's quite possible you will meet with opposition when writing and reviewing your child's IEP; and

3. to show that you should keep advocating for what you know is best for your child and never give up.

I have finally accepted that every new school year will create some new challenges to deal with, in addition to the challenges Ricochet tows with him from year to year. I've also accepted I'll have to keep advocating staunchly every single school year as the environment, players, and expectations of the game change with each new term.

Working with Your Child's Teacher

You now know there are a lot of players in the special education system and especially in creating your child's IEP. Of all of those potential players, however, I propose that it's your child's regular classroom teacher who determines success or failure, and whether your child gets special services and has an IEP or not. As far as regular classroom teachers go, we've had some real gems, and some real stinkers.

A great teacher for students with ADHD

An appropriate teacher for learning and behaviorally-challenged students will teach through differentiated instruction. This educational theory shapes the curriculum and instruction techniques to maximize learning for all students in the classroom, no matter their background knowledge, readiness, and preferences in learning style. This teacher will know that every child learns differently and at a varying pace and plan their lessons to accommodate for that. This teacher will work with your child's challenges rather than against them. This teacher's classroom feels safe and comfortable to a child with ADHD.

A terrible teacher for students with ADHD

On the flipside, a rigid teacher with a razor-sharp focus on the quantity of work is not a good match for a child with ADHD. This teacher prefers not to change or bend classroom systems and policies to accommodate a different learner. This teacher believes a special education student should not be given any "favors," such as fewer math problems for homework or extended time on tests. This teacher has set systems in place and is not willing to accommodate any needs that will require that they change. If your child is placed in a classroom with this teacher, request teacher re-assignment the minute you realize it. This teacher will inadvertently rob your child of every ounce of their self-esteem.

What does an equitable classroom look like?

Ricochet's first grade teacher, Mrs. Marvelous, is a precious pearl (she's so fantastic, she was named that school's *Teacher of the Year*). Mrs. Marvelous goes above and beyond to make sure she reaches all her students by creating an environment that incorporates all styles of learning. The approach creates a truly equitable classroom.

Following are her top ten techniques to incorporate children with ADHD seamlessly into a regular education classroom, while engaging all neurotypical children at the same time. Feel free to share these with your child's teachers.

1. The teacher should act as a facilitator in the classroom, providing appropriate tools and direction, but allowing the students to discover, problem-solve, and reach conclusions through visual, audio, and hands-on activity and peer interaction.

2. Provide multiple opportunities for engaging tasks, activities, or movement throughout the day. Make use of great resources like "Movin' to Math," an audio CD that combines music, exercise, and math. This incorporates learning, movement, and fun. Be sure to integrate as much technology as possible throughout the day as well. Most students have a lot of technology in their daily lives now and show more interest in it.

3. Use visual/picture cues whenever possible. Using visual reminders eliminates a constant disruption to class time to discuss rules. Students don't have to be embarrassed for inappropriate behavior; teachers can quietly point to the picture and redirect them without saying anything. Mrs. Marvelous wears a group of small illustrations on her lanyard, has larger versions to hold up during group lessons, and posts photos of current students successfully following the rules around her classroom (including my hyperactive son when he was in her class). These visual cues illustrate both negative and positive behaviors including: stop, good job, sitting, and raising your hand. While this system is for an early elementary classroom, it can be modified for older students as well. The teacher and student can collaborate to determine some discrete hand signals, and the teacher can simply place their hand on a student's shoulder to signal a need for return to focus.

Another great visual tool is the Time Timer®. This is a special timer that has a red disc that disappears with the passage of time, creating a visual of time elapsing and a constant but silent reminder of the amount of time remaining to complete a task. This works great for students with ADHD who often struggle with the concept of time. (It works well even at home to count down how long is left until time to set the table for dinner, for example.)

4. Provide a positive behavior model with 1-2 goals for the student to work on. For example, staying on task, taking your time with your independent work, staying in your own personal space, raising your hand, or saying "excuse me, please" before talking, etc. Provide a daily chart to work on these goals and reward often.

5. Praise students when caught doing well with the behaviors they are working to conquer. Positive praise is more effective behavior modification than calling out a student for doing something wrong. All kids want to be praised, and it's a powerful motivator. Work especially to recognize and praise those behaviors that are part of the student's personal behavior goals.

6. Provide multiple opportunities for students to do the talking. One method is *Focused Talk*, using the "turn and talk" technique to allow all voices to be heard in a positive, focused manner. In addition to offering the students an opportunity to learn from each other, *Focused Talk* gives them time to express themselves, all while teaching planning, social skills, debate, and problem-solving skills, and keeping it dynamic for active learners.

Focused Talk

Students are given a specific topic or question to discuss. Before directing them to turn and talk to their partner, provide a visual of ten fingers counting down for "private think time," ten seconds to gather their thoughts on the theme. Then instruct them to turn to their partner and discuss the topic. Each pair has a "talking stick," and they can only talk when holding the stick. The teacher then has the opportunity to listen in on the students' ideas and misconceptions. When talk time is up, count down 5, 4, 3, 2, 1 to signal it's time to come back together and focus as a class for teacher-lead discussion.

7. Give one-step directions, or give directions one step at a time. Children with ADHD have a hard time remembering multi-step directions and tend to feel overwhelmed by them as well. Simplify directions when possible and give longer, more complicated directions in stages and in writing.

8. Provide breaks after periods of work. Schedule recess after independent desk work, or use an interactive activity, like the Movin' to Math CD mentioned earlier, to provide a fun break after work. These breaks can be structured but shouldn't feel structured to the students. This is also a great time to incorporate occupational therapy activities for sensory needs.

9. Tailor accommodations to each individual child. What works for one child may not work for another. Each child learns differently and also has different goals to conquer their own tough behaviors.

10. Use music in the classroom throughout the day. Use music to signify and transition between each time block throughout the day for elementary students. This provides predictability and a natural time limit to decompress from the lesson and transition to the next task. For example, Mrs. Marvelous turns on *The Fox and the Chicken* after the morning announcements and pledge every day. Her students know it's time to clean up their morning work and take their place on the floor for carpet time before the song ends. She doesn't need to remind/pressure them to get finished — they are sort of racing the clock by racing to finish before the song does, even though the song provides plenty of time. She even makes her own CDs with song compilations that match the time she estimates for certain activities. Sometimes the music is just instrumental, sometimes not, depending on the activity it correlates with.

Ideal teachers for students with ADHD will integrate a child's special learning needs into all their classroom lessons and activities. In this type of classroom the same level of academic success is attainable by all. Encourage your school principal to place your child with ADHD into a classroom that implements differentiated instruction so they have a better opportunity to achieve academic success.

A Word About Private Schools

While you will think differently after reading this section, I am not against private schools. Many private schools are a much more experiential learning environment, which is often great placement for a student with ADHD. However, most private schools are not bound to the standards of IDEA and Section 504. You must tread very carefully when considering a private school for a child with ADHD.

IDEA only applies to private schools that receive a certain amount of federal funding. The same is true for Section 504. If the school doesn't receive federal dollars, they do not have to provide your special needs child with the accommodations necessary to level the educational playing field for them. Many do not have a special education department or even one special education teacher. That means your child may or may not get the small group or one-on-one instruction they need in certain areas. If they don't get it and the private school doesn't receive federal funds, then there's nothing you can do about it, other than move your child to another school.

Now, I think private schools that are designed for kids with ADHD and/or learning disabilities are fantastic. This is likely the best school you can choose for your child with ADHD, if this type of school is accessible to you.

If you are considering private school enrollment for your child with ADHD, please be careful and perform your due diligence before enrolling them. Read the school's handbook in full and ask for their special education or special learner's policy specifically. Be very up-front about your child's educational challenges before enrolling. We enrolled Ricochet in a small private school that practices experiential learning and has a strong science focus, knowing hands-on learning is best for him. I submitted every evaluation report, his last IEP, and his old 504 Plan to this school with his application for enrollment. I talked at length with the admissions director about Ricochet's learning challenges because I wanted to be very sure they could accommodate his needs. Despite all of that, this school accepted him, and he started at the beginning of his (first) fourth grade year. His classroom teacher told me she felt he needed a personal assistant after just one week. I was in meetings with the headmaster by week three and was told they couldn't teach Ricochet at their school after just seven weeks. It turned out that there was a clause in their handbook stating that they are not equipped to teach special needs children, but that handbook wasn't given to me before school started. Obviously, Ricochet was devastated, and so was I.

This momma has seen how private school and ADHD don't always mix — take extra precautions to make sure the private school you are considering is equipped and *willing* to handle your child's special educational needs. It's better to know that for certain up front than to do damage control on the back end.

Accommodations We've Found Useful

Ricochet has had different accommodations over the last six years in school, but there are some basics that are beneficial to most kids with ADHD.

In elementary school, permission to wiggle and move about is important for a child with ADHD with hyperactivity. Ricochet's first grade teacher put a rectangle on the floor around his desk with masking tape — when his peers were expected to attend quietly in their seats, Ricochet was permitted to move about his area as defined by the tape. He could lie on the floor under his desk to do his work, as long as his body and his belongings were within the taped rectangle.

Modified assignments is another important potential accommodation. As I discussed previously, a child with learning disabilities should only be expected to work as long as their neurotypical peers on homework. The length of time they invest is where there should be equality, not the volume of the workload. This applies to kids with ADHD of all ages if ADHD slows down their efficiency (due to distractibility and/or slow processing speed). Ricochet has a processing speed disproportionate to his IQ (processing is measured as part of some IQ tests), so he cannot complete the same volume of work in the same time as his neurotypical peers, or even as quickly as his IQ score might suggest. If this is a problem for your child as well, ask for modified assignments.

Extended time is also a common accommodation for students with ADHD and goes hand-in-hand with modified assignments. If your child has difficulty with completing tasks in the same time frame as his peers, or struggles with overwhelming anxiety under an impending deadline, ask for an extended time accommodation. This will allow them to take their time to do a good job, but will also accommodate for needing extra time due to distraction or poor processing speed.

Ricochet's therapist suggested he have access to a quiet area at school for completing work if he found himself distracted, and that's a good idea for all kids with ADHD. This could be a desk with a study carrel on top, a beanbag in the far corner of the classroom, or a separate room entirely. He goes to his resource teacher's room to complete tests or class work when he feels distracted.

Ricochet was also allowed to chew gum in school as an accommodation to improve focus and satisfy his extensive oral-sensory needs. Studies have shown that chewing gum improves focus, and the U.S. military often provides it to soldiers for that reason. I had to get special permission from the principal, and then it was placed in his 504 Plan originally, then his IEP. It was a big help with his obsessive sensory need to chew on something.

Of course, there are dozens more possibilities for classroom accommodations for students with ADHD. Think about what might help your child in the classroom, and then propose those items as potential accommodations to the teacher, IEP team, or even the principal. The accommodations list will look different for every child with ADHD.

Grades Aren't Everything

I was taught growing up that good grades were of the utmost importance and most definitely expected, as you may have been, too. If I received anything lower than a B on my report card, I received a punishment. I recall one or two C's but I worked as hard as I needed to earn A's and B's. "If you are smart, then you can make good grades," was the overwhelming philosophy in my house growing up. That is common sense, and my family didn't know any better — we didn't have any learning disabilities.

When Ricochet started receiving letter grades on his report cards in third grade, I was forced to adopt a new belief system about grades. My son is super-smart with a gifted-level IQ, but couldn't achieve all A's and B's. You *can* be smart, and try hard, and still not make good grades. It is possible and it does happen. That was new to me, but it made perfect sense in relation to what I knew about Ricochet, and I accepted it. He has had many C's on his report cards and a couple of D's too (one was actually an F, but that school didn't put F's on elementary kids' report cards). Mr. T and I know our son is smart and tries very hard to achieve the same academic success his peers do; that's what counts for him, not grades.

I imagine you are squirming in your chair right now at the thought of your child making crappy grades and feeling that will certainly mess up his future. That's not necessarily true. For one thing, elementary school grades do not get reported for college admissions, and I'm pretty sure middle school grades aren't either. High school is where grades really count if you want to go to college — but your child with ADHD may not go to college. If they do want to attend college though and haven't earned great grades, there are colleges with learning disabilities programs that will consider the whole of your child's academic challenges as part of the admissions process. Grades aren't everything.

Also, D's and F's on report cards are a sign of a student who has learning challenges and needs extra help in school, especially in the elementary years. If your child is really doing their best and still getting D's or F's, the school is not doing enough for them and they are not meeting your child's needs. Request a school meeting and talk about what else they can do to help your child in those areas.

Grades aren't everything (that bears repeating). The sooner you accept that your child may never make the honor roll, no matter how high his IQ, the better off you and your child will be. Grades are not a true measure of future success. These facts may help gain some perspective on ADHD, learning disabilities, and school: Einstein did terribly in school; Mark Twain dropped out of school at age thirteen; Quentin Tarantino dropped out of high school his freshman year; Peter Jennings got terrible grades in school; Stephen Spielberg was denied entry to a film school due to poor grades; Thomas Edison's teacher told him he was too stupid to learn anything... Grades really aren't everything. They sure aren't worth heartache and loss of self-worth, so don't push your special child too hard just for those ~~vile~~ silly little letters on report cards.

ADVOCACY BINDER

Make a Parent Advocacy Binder so you always have evaluation reports and your child's sample work at your fingertips for school incidents and meetings. Any kind of binder will do, but I'd get ~~one on wheels~~ a large one (I speak from experience). Keep pen or pencil and blank paper in the front pocket as well.

Always file the latest in front in every tab so you can easily reference the most updated information.

IEP or 504 PLANS

SCHOOL REPORTS

REPORT CARDS

PRIVATE EVALS

SAMPLE WORK

TAB 1 Current IEP or 504 Plan: Fill this area with all school plans, with the latest and greatest on top and then filed chronologically.

TAB 2 School Evaluation Reports: This includes all the testing results and reporting done by the school.

TAB 3 Report Cards: In my opinion, report cards are the most useful measure of academic success, whether the school considers that true or not. That shows what your child is capable of doing in a classroom setting with the current level of accommodations. When they use achievement testing to show academic achievement, that shows what your child can do one-on-one in a quiet setting with lots of prompts. It's completely different. It's important to have current grades on hand throughout the school year.

TAB 4 Private Evaluation Reports: This is where you file reports from private doctors, therapists, lab work, occupational therapists, etc.

TAB 5 Samples of Student's Work: File samples of your child's work that you find indicative of their current needs. Once the school year is completed, take the sample work out for the prior year and file it somewhere else. Trust me, you do not have room in the binder nor the stamina to build that up and lug it around year after year.

There are other things you may want to keep in the binder, too. You can certainly add a poly-envelope to hold loose items. I also recommend adding various articles that you might need to share with teachers and school staff. Try to limit it to a few short articles on the finer details of ADHD, such as executive functioning and inconsistency in behavior and attention.

Finally, in front of Tab 1, put letters your child has written to the team and letters you've written to the school on your child's behalf. These could be letters of introduction for a new teacher, letters to address an issue and ask for accommodations, etc.

P/T COMMUNICATION FORM

STUDENT'S NAME _____

CLASSROOM GOALS	MATH	SCIENCE	ENGLISH	S.S.

OTHER GOAL AREAS
(recess, gym, lunch)

Place smiles here, when earned.

_____

_____

_____

TEACHER INITIALS

MATH ____   SCIENCE ____   ENGLISH ____   S.S. ____

TEACHER COMMENTS   PARENT COMMENTS

NOTE: Teacher should place a smiley face when the student meets that particular goal. If they did not, just leave it BLANK. Do **not** place an X or write "No" in the blank. This is for positive reinforcement. If you or the teacher need to discuss a weakness or negative behavior, the comments should include that a private email or phone call is in order.

Sample Letters

There are often times when you need to write a formal letter to your child's school. Use the sample letters on the following pages to guide you when drafting letters to the school about your child's educational needs. I have provided only a few here, but a quick Google search will produce sample letters on a multitude of subjects.

Letter to Introduce Your Child to Their Teachers: SAMPLE

[Date]

Dear [Teachers' Names],

Over the years, we have found it helpful to give teachers some background about [your child's name], in addition to the [IEP or 504] in his student file. This often ensures a successful beginning to the school year.

[Your child's name] has attention deficit hyperactivity disorder (ADHD). He is on medication, but it is more effective at helping him focus than at controlling his behavior. [Your child's name] has a great sense of humor, and tapping into this early in the year usually works well. [Your child's name] takes criticism personally and hates being scolded. He won't always let you know it, but he worries and is very sensitive. He might try to act tough, but, if he has had a bad day, he falls apart when he gets home.

[Your child's name] loves [science] and also excels at [math and problem solving]. He is excited about the new year and starting [what grade]. He wants school to go well so he doesn't have to be so worried there every day. He always has the best intentions, but he can't always succeed. The last couple of school years were difficult, and [your child's name]'s self-esteem has been damaged.

Included is a letter directly from [your child's name] about himself and what he would like your help with.

We welcome any ideas you have to keep [your child's name] engaged in school, while boosting his self-esteem and helping him succeed. Please contact us at any time by phone or e-mail. We look forward to working with you in the upcoming year.

Sincerely,

[Parents' names]

Letter Requesting a School Evaluation: SAMPLE

[Your Name and Contact information]

[Date]

[School Name + Address]

Re: [Your child's name and date of birth]

Dear [Administrator Name],

I am the parent of [your child's name] who is a student in [teacher's name]'s [grade] class at [Name of School]. [Your child's name] was recently diagnosed with attention-deficit hyperactivity disorder (ADHD). I have attached the report from [doctor's name and office name], who made the ADHD diagnosis. Please be sure that all teachers who have [your child's name] in their classroom (music, PE, art, etc.) are provided a copy of the enclosed report.

Since [your child's name] entered school, teachers have been raising concerns about his academic performance and behavior. He is not meeting his potential in school, despite the efforts of [teacher's name] to create an environment in which he can thrive. He may need special education services. Therefore, I wish to request that you consider the doctor's report and assess my child for appropriate educational services and interventions according to the provisions of Section 504 of the Rehabilitation Act and the IDEA laws.

I look forward to hearing from you and working further with you to ensure a successful educational experience for [your child's name]. Please provide copies of your assessment results at least three days prior to any meetings at which these results would be discussed.

Sincerely,

[Your Name]

Cc: [other administrators] and [classroom teacher]

Letter Opposing School Decision

[Your Name and Contact information]

[Date]

[School Name + Address]

Re: [Your child's name and date of birth]

Dear [Administrator Name],

I am the parent of [your child's name] who is a student in [teacher's name]'s [grade] class at [Name of School]. I am writing to request an Independent Educational Evaluation (IEE) at public expense for the following reasons:

[Give a quick synopsis of why you disagree with the school evaluation results and/or the denial of special education inclusion. If referencing particular reports or test scores, be sure to list the evaluator's name, the exact title of the test or report, and the date of the test or report. For example:

I disagree with the school evaluation completed on 11/11/11 by Mrs. So-and-So. My child has shown a history of struggling to achieve grade level in reading, yet the school evaluation states that my child is on grade level in all subjects. Furthermore, in an evaluation at Smith Behavioral Health Center on 10/10/11, Dr. So-and-So diagnosed my child with dyslexia.]

I look forward to hearing from you at your earliest convenience. Prompt attention to this matter is crucial to ensure a successful educational experience for [your child's name].

Sincerely,

[Your Name]

Cc: [other administrators], [classroom teacher], and [special education teacher]

Take Care of You!

Parents do a whole lot for others but rarely for themselves, especially moms. It is imperative that we also take time for ourselves. This is a lesson I still haven't implemented fully, but I'm making a concerted effort. The oxygen mask theory applies — you must put the oxygen mask on yourself first before you are capable of helping others to your full potential. Taking time for yourself does not have to be time-consuming or costly. You could take a walk alone each day, set aside a bit of time for a hobby each week, get a massage or a manicure every now and then, take a nightly bubble bath, have girls' or guys' night with your friends regularly, etc.

Don't make excuses to postpone your own self-care. (*Yeah, Penny!*) If you wait for available time, you will never have time for yourself. Create opportunities for yourself; make it a regular part of your family schedule if you have to. If you are exhausted and burned out, you can't do your best for others and especially not for yourself. Keep in mind too, chronically stressed parents (women especially) are much more likely to develop physical and mental health problems. Self-care is crucial, especially when you lead a stressful life like parents of kids with ADHD do.

Think it through carefully before you accept a particular task as self-care. Here's a list of tasks that might feel like they are for you, but which are deceptive and are not part of self-care. Avoid these during your allotted time for self-care:

› Creating the weekly menu (it does make life easier when you're the primary cook, but it's not self-care)

› Making a formal grocery list (again, it does make life easier when you're the primary shopper, but it's not self-care)

› Running to the store by yourself for more dishwasher soap

> › Washing even your own laundry

> › Finally cleaning out the refrigerator after it's been driving you
> crazy for months

When I use the term self-care, I mean the restorative kind of care
— think chocolate, bubble baths, a glass of wine, a facial, an afternoon
golfing, etc. — whatever causes your muscles to relax and your brain to let
out a big sigh of relief. Do that and do it often.

Taking time to decompress benefits your mind, body, and spirit, then
consequently benefits your family, too. What's the saying, "Happy wife,
happy life"? How about "Happy momma, less drama!" Or, "Happy dad,
we're all glad!" You deserve to be happy, too — make it happen.

MOMMA SELF-CARE

List ideas of things you can do to take care of yourself. These *must* be incorporated into your daily life, and frequently.

Sign up for a music, art, dance, or exercise class.
Get a MASSAGE or a SPA PEDICURE

TAKE walks alone
a scenic drive
bubble baths

GET TOGETHER
W/FRIENDS!

listen to your own needs

PRACTICE
mindfulness

laugh

Make At-Home Spa Treatments & Pamper yourself

DREAM BIG

>> _____

>> _____

>> _____

>> _____

>> _____

>> _____

Step 8: Get a Handle on ADHD at Home

>>>>>>>>>>>>

"That's what people do who love you. They put their arms around you and love you when you're not so lovable."

—Deb Caletti

Most parents of children with ADHD, myself included, tend to worry about effective treatment of their child's ADHD during the school year and during school hours more than any other time. By focusing only on successful treatment for school though, we are accepting a tough family atmosphere at home — and we shouldn't. We must seek the best possible ADHD management during all hours of all days for our kids with ADHD — for their success, happiness, and self-esteem. A positive home environment is just as important as a positive school experience for our kids, maybe even more so. Use all the tools in your ADHD toolbox to create a beneficial home life, too.

#1 Rule, Remain Calm

Here it is again, the #1 rule of parenting a child with ADHD — remain calm. It's so important that I repeat it ~~incessantly~~ again and again throughout this book.

Simply making a concerted effort to always remain calm with your child with ADHD will cause a dramatic shift in your family dynamic, and your relationship with your child. There are many more strategies to implement at home when parenting a child with ADHD, but this one is, by far, the most effective overall.

I will start this section on remaining calm with a personal confession — I still raise my voice to Ricochet sometimes (and the rest of the family as well). I didn't say remaining calm is easy, I merely said it is the most important strategy. Raising my voice only sometimes is a whole lot less than the frequency Ricochet used to experience. Seeking calm in the face of ADHD has provided positive differences I now see in myself, our family, and, most importantly, in Ricochet. It has truly shifted our family dynamic in a very beneficial way.

Before Ricochet's diagnosis six years ago, he probably heard, "Why can't you just…" multiple times each and every day (if he even heard what I said at all). He experienced someone raising their voice to him or using a stern tone at least once a day as well, multiple times most days. His undesirable behaviors looked like nothing more than willful little boy defiance to us — it felt like he was not complying with parental requests just to get a rise. Mr. T and I punished, we yelled, we mucked around in a deep sea of frustration that was rapidly becoming quicksand. Home life felt awful for all of us, even Warrior Girl. It was always loud and tense and uncomfortable. We didn't yet know there was another way, a more appropriate way to parent this child.

Most children with ADHD have very little frustration tolerance, and many are also quite inflexible. Those two things are the underlying triggers of most unwanted behavior in a nutshell.

Once Ricochet was diagnosed, I quickly submersed myself in all things ADHD. I read every book I could. I spent countless hours on the Internet researching. I stalked online forums to hear real-life parenting experiences as they related to ADHD. I wanted to know how to help my son, and I wanted to know right away.

It didn't take long for me to realize we were punishing him and yelling in instances that were not within his control at that time. I immediately made a conscious effort to not get riled up about ADHD behaviors. Easier said than done, but I was determined. In my fear of punishing Ricochet for behaviors he couldn't control, I swung too far in the opposite direction and began using ADHD as an excuse for everything. That too was no way to parent this kid. He began to feel like it didn't matter

> *Simply making a concerted effort to always remain calm with your child with ADHD will cause a dramatic shift in your family dynamic, and your relationship with your child.*

what he did because he could simply blame it on ADHD and all would be forgiven.

Then, about two years after his diagnosis, I read the book *The Explosive Child: A New Approach for Understanding and Parenting Easily Frustrated, Chronically Inflexible Children*, by Dr. Ross Greene. No, Ricochet is not explosive, but Greene's book, *Lost at School*, provided such a common-sense explanation for meltdowns that I had to read his other title, too. Reading *The Explosive Child* is, hands down, one of the best things I have done to date for Ricochet, and for our family. It opens a perspective on the process of frustration in these children that so perfectly explains the nuances of my child (and children with ADHD in general). This entire book was my ah-ha moment of that decade!

Now I had the knowledge to stop yelling at my son and work with him instead to resolve negative behaviors. Here are the steps to achieve more calm in the face of raising a child with ADHD:

1. **Recognize that what looks like willful disobedience may not be.**
   The first step is to truly understand your child with ADHD and why they do the things they do (we learned this in *Step 4: Get to Know Your Child*), especially those things that look and feel like willful

disobedience. Believe it or not, sometimes it can look like a duck and quack like a duck, but turn out to be a goat. I'm not saying that a child with ADHD is a goat doesn't have moments of willful disobedience like any other child; I am saying they are no more frequent than a neurotypical child, despite seeming so. Most children with ADHD have very little frustration tolerance, and many are also quite inflexible. Those two things are the underlying triggers of most unwanted behavior in a nutshell.

2. **Guide them through frustration.** How many times has your child asked for something and then completely melted down when they didn't get it? When they are two or three years old, you expect that. When they are eight or nine years old, you think they should know better. You try to impose your will and put your foot down, and they spiral out of control. You think it's all because they didn't get their way. But it's not. That's right, they're not throwing a fit to strong-arm you into giving them what they want — it's not even a "fit" in that sense at all. They melt down because they don't have the skills to see that there's more than one option, and they don't have the skills to handle the frustration they feel when the one and only thing they know to be true in that moment isn't.

Here's a simplistic example we neurotypical parents can understand: You're on your way to the grocery store in your car. You pull into the center turn lane to turn left into the parking lot. Then you realize that the entrance is blocked off for road construction. You need to go to the grocery store right now, but you can't access it your usual way. You and I would probably merge back into traffic and continue on to look for another entrance, or even park at a neighboring business and walk over to the store. But, for "easily frustrated, chronically inflexible" kids, they are stuck in the turn lane with their signal on, and panic and frustration ensue because they can't access the store. All they see at that moment is the grocery store behind a blocked entrance. They don't inherently possess the skills to automatically problem-solve and find an alternate acceptable solution in that moment. Happily, we can teach these skills through repetition, role-

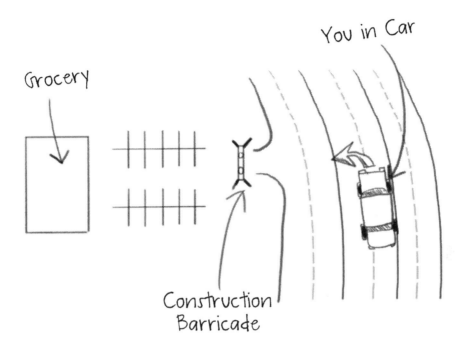

play, and helping them brainstorm to determine a solution.

Part of understanding why they do the things they do is also watching for triggers, as we discussed in Step 4: Get to Know Your Child. I watched very closely when Ricochet's behavior was undesirable and took note of the physical environment, if he was tired or hungry, and what had taken place just before. You will begin to see a pattern as I did and be able to make adjustments to attempt to prevent some undesirable outcomes. Preventing these outcomes will naturally prevent the need to raise your voice.

You must not engage, but remain detached in these situations. You do that by remembering that your child's behavior, as much as it may seem so sometimes, is not a personal attack on you. By not taking it personally, you have a much better chance of staying calm.

Recently, Ricochet had a meltdown at the grocery store because I wouldn't buy him the cheesy popcorn he wanted (that I'd bought him two days before and he inhaled in 30 minutes). I reminded him that I picked up two items not on my list already because he requested them and that was all I could do that day. "I hate you" and "You don't love me" and "I'm gonna run away tonight" deflected off the ceiling and echoed up and down every aisle of the store. I could have engaged and given him an ultimatum to stop or else — but I didn't. I chose to detach and not take it personally. By not believing his insults, I didn't get riled up, but instead remained calm. I shopped a bit quicker, but I didn't threaten, I didn't punish, and I didn't yell, because I knew he didn't have the skills to handle the fact that his request was unmet. The meltdown was much shorter because I understood the source and remained calm. Once he was calm again as well, we talked about how there are many other days in our future that we can buy cheesy popcorn — that day was not the one and only day we would have the opportunity to purchase his favorite snack again.

3. **Work together and teach your child with ADHD lagging skills** in these moments. If your child is frustrated because their playdate is cancelled, talk through the situation with them. Show empathy for how they are feeling. Talk about when you could reschedule it and what they might do when they get the opportunity to finally play with that child. Talk about what you might do with the original time instead, now that it's free. This not only teaches them to think through options, but it distracts both of you from being emotional about the situation. View everything as a problem to

> *Don't relinquish control to your child or to an undesirable situation.*

be solved, and take the opportunity to teach problem-solving skills. (Playing strategy games like chess and many others is a great way to teach problem-solving skills, too.)

4. **Lastly, remember who really has control of the situation — you, the parent** — even when it feels like your child is trying to control you. Don't relinquish control to your child or to an undesirable situation. There are plenty of ways to regain control and authority besides raising your voice or laying down a mandate. In fact, engaging by raising your voice or threatening punishment if they don't act right will prolong the outburst, but remaining calm and detached will actually shorten it.

Some other ideas to prevent yourself from yelling:

> sing a song or hum a tune in your head to distract yourself

> walk away from your child until they're calm (be careful, sometimes this escalates a meltdown)

> redirect their attention

> go into another room, close the door, and yell into your pillow instead of at your child

Manage Expectations

We already established that kids with ADHD need structure to do well. Routines provide great structure and define expectations for household tasks. Create a routine for everything that happens in your home: entering the house, exiting the house, doing the laundry, washing the dog, loading the dishwasher, completing homework, mowing the yard, taking out the trash, cleaning your room — if each task is done the same way each time, your child knows what is expected of them and how to succeed at meeting your expectations. Post step-by-step lists for each task to make it as simple as possible while they are learning the family's systems.

As I discussed already in *Step 5: Make a Plan*, you should create and post house rules as well. This also defines expectations and offers opportunities for calm.

Planning and Organization

Planning and organization are a huge challenge for those with ADHD. Add in the immaturity, lack of motivation, and just plain "I don't care if it's clean" attitude of most children and you have one heck of a mess.

You need to be the glue that keeps them together, at least until they learn the skills to implement planning and organization strategies themselves. Implementing structure through routines and a published schedule, as previously discussed in *Step 3: Create Structure* and above in *Manage Expectations*, is a great starting point for teaching planning and organization skills. Involving your child in creating the schedule and routines is key — they are then learning by doing, which is one of the best learning methods for kids with ADHD.

A mess makes me crazy. Really, really crazy! In my brain, every object has a home and should never be set down anywhere but in its rightful place. I live with two children and a husband who cultivate a disheveled environment though. They are the anti to my order. They just don't see the mess — it doesn't bother them, and so it doesn't even register that there might be a problem. That is extremely problematic for me.

For years, I have been cleaning up behind everyone because I just can't stand it. But no sooner would I tidy up one corner and move on to the next than I'd turn around and find that first corner again a disaster. That is so very frustrating, as you can imagine. I'm sure you experience that with kids yourself.

Cleaning and organizing for them, without involving them in the process, doesn't help them at all. In fact, it enables them to continue to be a disorganized mess. It's a lot more work to involve them and talk through every minuscule step, but that's the only way they will learn organization skills themselves.

When I work on organizational skills with Ricochet, we walk through every step together, both physically and verbally. I let him lead the process while I facilitate. I ask, "Where do you think is a good place to keep your winter hat and gloves?" for instance. This forces him to think it through and make a decision, which is the organizational process. We will have to clean up and organize together like this for years, but the organizing process will become deep-rooted over time.

> You need to be the glue that keeps them together, at least until they learn the skills to implement planning and organization strategies themselves.

In 2009, I decided it was time to start teaching my kids organization and I came up with a plan. I realized I had to make it as easy as possible to maintain order — break the process down into small increments — and enforce a daily quick tidy so that it never became overwhelming again. Feeling overwhelmed is the source of many an ADHD meltdown and tons of procrastination. Feeling overwhelmed and not knowing where to start is one of the biggest hurdles to being organized when you have ADHD. While I haven't been successful at enforcing the daily quick-tidy, I only pick up a small amount behind my kids now, when I had been picking up almost everything for them for years. It's tough to take the time to take advantage of so many teachable moments, but it means a world of difference for your kids with ADHD. (Not now — right now they hate you for making them do "everything" for themselves, but you will see the benefits in a few years.)

Following are some recommended organizational systems that have worked well for our family and/or for others:

Toy Storage

In the Great Williams Simplification Reorganization of 2009, I completely revamped Ricochet's toy storage, which resides in his bedroom. He had four large plastic tubs I bought when he was about three years old. While it looked cohesive aesthetically because they were all the same size and color, every time Ricochet wanted a specific toy he had to dump the buckets on the floor until he found what he was after. Once a bucket was dumped, the large scale of the mess was too overwhelming for him to clean up.

I thought the tubs were organized enough, but, as I learned more about ADHD and Ricochet's specific struggles, I realized we needed to sort toys into smaller, more manageable groups and tidy each day to keep the unwelcome task short and simple. The new cubby and bin system was a little expensive, but it made a world of difference and continues to be well worth the investment.

I used a modular system that could be customized to Ricochet's exact needs and modified as his storage needs change. I started by making a list of all the categories I could sort Ricochet's toys into and whether each required a small, medium, or large bin. Our categories were:

> Hot Wheels cars

> Medium-sized toy cars

> Trains

> K'Nex

> Action figures

> Animal and dinosaur figures

> *Toy Story* action figures (he has a big set of these)

> Stuffed animals

> Writing/drawing

> Flying toys (Nerf gun, fly wheels, etc.)

> Balls

> Army figures

> Misc.

He has lots of bins, but they are sorted into manageable amounts of toys and labeled. He can quickly scan and find what he wants without removing anything he doesn't want. He has been a lot less frustrated with this new storage system for sure.

Plus, he can pull out the entire bin and take it to a play area. When he's done, he just drops the toys back in the bin quickly and puts it back on the shelf. So fast and simple! And so manageable.

This toy storage system does not prevent a mess on its own. Once his room starts to get messy (mostly by things he brings in and drops down instead of taking the extra minute to put away), it's easy for him to stop putting things in appropriate bins altogether and just drop everything inside the doorway. Admittedly, I don't implement a quick tidy often enough to keep his room as clean and organized as it should be. But now that he has manageable categories of toys, it is leaps and bounds better than it was.

Entry/Exit System

In our old house, we had a cubby system Mr. T, the woodworker, built in our entryway for organizing all things you enter and exit the house with. There was a long bench where the lid could be lifted to reveal cubbies to keep shoes in. There were doors that concealed hooks for coats and a ledge for purses and backpacks. And there were cubby openings at the top with a basket in each for gloves, hats, and scarves. There were four of every cubby type, so each family member had their own space. When you entered the house, you went to the cubby and kicked off your shoes, hung your coat, put away your backpack, keys, hats, gloves, etc. Then, when it was time to go somewhere, we didn't have to search high and low all over the house for a missing shoe or car keys. It was all right there by the door — so simple and yet genius. I definitely miss that mudroom type of build-out now.

You can recreate the entry/exit organizational system without having an elaborate built-in at your entry or mudroom though. Our current home didn't have space to create built-in cubbies for each family member, so I retrofitted the coat closet. I put shoe organizers on the floor of the closet and all shoes go there. I put the baskets for hats and gloves we had at the old house on the shelf of the coat closet — during the winter I relocate them under a small entry table by the door so the kids can reach them. Of course, coats hang in the coat closet, and backpacks usually rest in the closet floor with the shoes. I hung a key rack behind the garage door where we typically enter and exit the house. It's all located within a 4-foot radius from the door.

If you enter and exit the house through multiple areas, I suggest a bin to contain shoes by every exterior door. Ricochet comes in and out the front door a lot during the summer while playing with neighbors. That causes him to kick off his shoes somewhere in the front of the house and leave them wherever that happens to be because he's not entering and exiting the house by the coat closet as usual. A bin or basket by the front entry would certainly be smart for us, too.

You'll enjoy the benefit of reclaiming some time when family members don't have to look all through the house for items they need on their way out the door. That is, as long as they all utilize the entry/exit system as intended. You'll need to remind everyone to use the system when you first implement it, but you won't have to do that forever (hopefully).

Color Coding for Organization

Most individuals with ADHD are very visual learners and thinkers. They need to be able to glance at something and get the essential information right away. One great visual method of organizing tasks and information is by color coding.

For kids, the best opportunity for color-coded organization is to code things by category for school. If your child has a folder or notebook for each subject, assign a color to each subject and then get all supplies for that subject in the corresponding assigned color. If the school requests specific colors for each subject/class, you can go with those colors if they make sense to your child, or affix colored stickers to each item in the color scheme your child chose.

Let your child select the color for each subject so they can use associations that make sense to them to remember the subject-color combination. Ricochet hasn't had different notebooks or folders for different subjects yet, but Warrior Girl uses this system. She chose red for math because she hates math, green for science because lots of nature is green, and blue for art class because blue is her favorite color and art is her favorite subject. It helps to organize visually for all ages, but this system has a secondary benefit for kids with lockers as well. Students with lockers have a very limited amount of time between classes to retrieve the correct supplies for their next class. If they just have to grab everything red (cover their books in coordinating colors, too), it will be so much easier to get the right supplies and all the necessary supplies before heading to the next class. That eliminates some of the stress for them, especially those with slow processing speed, like Ricochet.

A Central HUB for Electronics

There are a *lot* of handheld and portable electronic devices in our immediate family. We each have an iPhone or iPod, a tablet, and a laptop computer. The kids also each have a Nintendo 3DS and a PSP. That means a whole lot of charging needs to happen each night while we sleep.

At first, we allowed the kids to be in charge of their own power cords. Ricochet would invariably lose his and then come thieve ours. As well, he never had a charged device because he never remembered to plug them in when he wasn't using them (that I-can-only-think-of-the-here-and-now ADHD trait). This quickly became a source of tension and arguments in our house, but having charged electronics really didn't have to be so taxing.

At Ricochet's counselor's urging, I made a central hub for charging the kids' electronics. I purchased replacements for all missing and damaged cords and a power strip with additional U.S.B plugs for our charging hub. I picked a central spot in the house and set up the cords where devices could be plugged in to charge, then laid on a flat surface securely. Before going to bed, Ricochet has to plug in all his devices and leave them in this location until morning. When something dies during the day, he is to plug it in there until there's enough battery to play it without the cord again. We no longer have lost cords and we certainly don't have any that have been mindlessly shredded with his teeth {gasp!} while playing a game. It solved a consistent irritation and a safety issue and saves us a lot of ~~sanity~~ time that we were spending looking for missing charge cords.

Chore Center

I have seen many chore systems I know would work well for kids with ADHD. If your kids have several daily or weekly chores, create a system to track what has been completed and what still needs to be done. A visual system and a way of "putting away" a chore after it is done will keep your child with ADHD from being too overwhelmed.

My favorite system for chores is a magnet board. Create a magnet with a picture and written title for each chore (you can print the pictures from the Internet and buy magnet sheets with adhesive from the craft store). Next, on a magnetic board, create a column for a parking lot (for chores that don't need to be done at that time), columns for each child, and then a column for completed chores. The chore magnets rest in the parking lot when not being used. When a chore is assigned to a child, the magnet for that chore is moved into that child's column. When they have completed the chore, they will move the associated chore magnet out of their column and into the completed chores column. At the end of each day for a daily chart, or the end of each week for a weekly chart, move all the magnets from the completed chores column back into the parking lot and into assignment columns again. What I find more useful about this chore system is that each child can see exactly how much "work" they have to do and they can see their progress as there are less and less magnets in their column. This prevents your child from telling you that they've already done "a hundred things" and they can't do any more — you have a visual to keep them rational.

I have also seen a similar chore system using tongue depressors or Popsicle sticks. You cut out the picture (I would laminate them too), glue it to the top of the stick, and write the title of the chore on the stick. All the chore sticks can reside standing in a cup, and appropriate chore sticks can be moved into each child's personal cup as their to-do list. Once the chore is completed, they can then move that chore stick to another cup that holds completed chores. Some families leave all the chores for the day in the one cup together, and the kids choose a chore from the cup and put the chore stick into their own cup when it's completed. This would motivate your children to get their chores done quickly if they want a say in what chores they have to do, as I'm sure that system would cause some competition for the more desirable chores. (I imagine changing the cat's litter box would always be the last chore stick in the To-Do cup.) Under that system, all chores need to require an equal amount of effort though and must be age-appropriate for all your children.

When creating organizational systems for kids with ADHD, remember to keep it very simple *and intuitive to their age of maturity*, not their chronological age. As well, walk through the process of using these systems with your child over and over again until each becomes habit for them.

Surviving Mornings with a Child with ADHD

Mornings are a bear for many people, but especially for an individual with ADHD. Well, my child, who has ADHD and SPD, acts like a bear most mornings. He was more like an angry ~~devil-child~~ monster in the mornings when he was younger, but, as he started to mature, he learned our morning routine and became more pleasant and cooperative at that time, promoting him to just a bear. Most mornings now I'd even give him cute bear cub status — it took a lot of structure and routine reiterated every day, but we improved our mornings dramatically, and you can too.

"The school morning routine is one of the most difficult areas for ADHD children," says Betsy Corrin, PhD, a child psychologist at Packard Children's Hospital and the Stanford University School of Medicine in the article, "Minimize School Morning Mayhem for ADHD Children," on *WebMD.com*. "The morning is time-pressured and involves a lot of steps. And such stressful situations don't bring out the best in many ADHD kids or their parents," says Corrin[21].

So how do we get our kids with ADHD out the door with our patience and sanity still intact? Implement the following strategies each morning:

Behavior Charts

Your first inclination may be to implement a behavior chart and reward system. That's likely what your therapist or that other book on ADHD recommended, after all. But there's a huge disconnect here between what most

ADHD experts tell us (to use lots of behavior charts) and what can be helpful for children with ADHD in real, everyday life. Reward chart systems are *not* effective for most children with ADHD, because impulsivity prevents them from weighing consequences and rewards before acting, especially when they have to earn the reward over a period of time.

However, a morning routine checklist is one time I've had success with a behavior chart with Ricochet — my low success rate prior was not due to ~~desperation~~ a lack of trying either. This was more of a checklist than a reward chart; he was rewarded as soon as he finished the list every morning.

I typed up an inventory of every item he needed to complete to be ready to leave for school in the mornings, even eating breakfast. I kept it to a 4x6-inch size for easy manageability, then laminated it and put a paperclip on the side. The paperclip pointed to the item he was currently working on. He carried the card with him and moved the clip down each time he completed a task so it would point to the next task. He felt like it was a game and was happy to follow the list. The last task read, "If complete by 7:20 AM, you may play electronics."

In all honesty, we lost the checklist a long time ago, but this morning checklist worked great when Ricochet was younger. He truly doesn't need this sort of checklist now, because the steps to the morning routine became habit by using the structured list consistently early on. Mornings are now much easier. Not easy, but much easier.

Visuals are crucial to a majority of kids with ADHD, especially if they endure slow processing speed or poor working memory. Creating a visual morning checklist, one with a picture for each step, can be helpful for many kids with ADHD, too.

```
Morning Routine: RICOCHET
☐ Get dressed

☐ Pajamas in dirty clothes basket

☐ Brush teeth

☐ Swish mouth wash

☐ Make breakfast choice

☐ Make lunch choice

☐ Eat Breakfast

☆ If complete before 7:20 am and breakfast
is eaten, you may use electronics.
```

Wake Them Gently

Ripping off the covers and flooding the room with piercing light will surely put anyone in a bad mood. This is certainly not how you want to start off the day with a child with ADHD. Allow plenty of extra time each morning for slow waking. If Ricochet is not already up before me, I will try tickling him to wake up — laughter is always welcome. His dog also likes to jump up on the bed and nudge and lick him, which is very helpful; it's hard to sleep through a hot, wet goo of slobber being smeared all over your face.

Our counselor recommends kids with ADHD set their own alarm and for a time at least twenty minutes before they have to get up. That will remove the bad mood blame-game and teach them the skills they will need when they are living on their own. We tried an alarm clock in Ricochet's room for a brief while when he was eight, but he slept right through the alarm. The rest of us were jolted out of the bed early, and I still had the unpleasant task of waking him, so we stopped setting his alarm. I have seen products that are supposed to help even the toughest morning riser get out of bed — clocks on wheels that you have to chase to turn off and daylight simulators that light the room slowly over time, like the sun rising. If your child is difficult to wake, you might try their own alarm clock or the clock on wheels (called Clocky). If they do best waking slowly, give a daylight simulator alarm clock a try. I plan to try an alarm clock in Ricochet's room again when he's twelve or thirteen years old — he has to learn to wake himself and get ready at some point, and I think that's a good age to try again.

Create the Appropriate Environment

It's very important to control your child's environment during the morning to help create a positive start to their day. First, don't allow them to watch television unless they are ready to walk out the door with time to spare. My son can't eat when the TV is on, and he surely can't walk away to get dressed or brush his teeth. The TV is a big no-no, but music playing in the background could be helpful. As well, don't turn on a bunch of bright lights right away. Use soft lamps or indirect light to illuminate just as much as is necessary. Avoid fluorescent lights, too; they are harsh and irritating to most kids with sensory issues, including many kids with ADHD. Keep light and noise low and eliminate the possibility of distraction during your morning routine.

Prepare the Night Before

The less pressure each morning the better. Do as much prep work as possible the night before to reduce the number of decisions that your child will need to make under the stress of time constraints: lay out clothing, place shoes by the door, pack their book bag, pack their lunch, choose what they'll eat for breakfast, and even put the toothpaste on the toothbrush, all before going to bed the night before (this can all be part of your bedtime routine). Planning ahead will minimize the scope of tasks they need to manage under the pressure of having limited time to get ready. This should minimize the opportunities for morning meltdowns.

Be Flexible About Breakfast

As I stated prior, it generally takes a lot more effort for a child with ADHD to make decisions. Planning what they'll eat for breakfast the night before might help, but they may just change their mind in the morning anyway. If you can convince your child to eat the same breakfast every morning, it removes decision-making from the equation and makes breakfast easier for child and parent alike. One school year, Ricochet and Warrior Girl drank a protein shake every morning in lieu of a traditional breakfast, although they eventually grew tired of it. Even though making shakes every morning was a lot of effort, it was still much easier than trying to drag a decision out of my half-asleep, clinically-indecisive child and his picky sister. And shakes are 100 percent portable if you're running late.

Any portable food is a good idea for chaotic mornings actually. If your child is okay with eating in the car (and you are ok with letting them ~~spill~~ eat in your car), let them have breakfast on the way to school. At that point they are ~~hostages~~ a captive audience and won't have anything else to do but eat their breakfast. If they ride the bus to school, let them take their breakfast and eat it on the walk to the bus stop. You can definitely feed them a nutritious breakfast in a portable format: protein shakes, yogurt smoothies, fruit smoothies, yogurt tubes, breakfast burrito, apple, banana, breakfast sandwich, protein bars, cheese, etc. are all nutritious and portable.

If your child wakes hungry and before you, create a breakfast basket to leave out on the kitchen counter. Fill the basket with a variety of items that are appropriate choices for breakfast. We implemented this recently because Ricochet was waking before us, raiding the kitchen in extreme hunger, and consuming a lot of inappropriate foods (like ¾ of a tub of ice cream). The breakfast basket allows him the power to choose what to eat, but I still have control over the choices, too.

Provide Movement Time

Exercise is proven to be very helpful to those with ADHD. Sustained elevated heart rate increases blood flow to the brain, often causing it to function more efficiently. Before leaving for school, allow your child 10-20 minutes to go outside and play, walk the dog, jump on an outdoor trampoline or a mini-trampoline indoors, or, as Ricochet does some mornings, run laps around the living room. Or how about a morning dance party to inject energy and inspire good spirits? Anything goes here as long as it's safe and it gets them moving continually for ten minutes or more.

Remain Calm

I know I have said this at least twice already, and recently, but it is so important it bears repeating again and again: Remaining calm is the #1 most important thing, truly. You must remain calm at all times with a child with ADHD. This is a challenge for sure and one I am not completely successful with, but I try with all my might to remain calm. Yelling or threatening only escalates emotional reactions and causes more harm than good. Ask your child to stop for a moment and look you in the eye, then very calmly and softly tell them what you need them to do and what the consequence will be if they aren't on task.

Set a good example — if you are anxious or angry, they will be too. Don't be reactive, be proactive.

Homework Help

We have established that children with ADHD do better with structure and routines. It's a proven fact. In a brain characteristically in chaos, the order routine provides is necessary and soothing. They need to know what to expect in advance and have time to make the mental transition as well.

Everything goes more smoothly for Ricochet when he knows what's coming and when. Conversely, everything falls apart when our schedule changes unexpectedly. As parents of neurologically different children, we make their world more comfortable by publicizing the family schedule and sticking to routines as much as a family can. We have a routine for getting up and ready for school in the morning, and we have a bedtime routine as well. We even have an {unpopular} dinnertime routine. Why should homework time be any different?

It took me two years after Ricochet's diagnosis to establish a fairly comfortable homework routine for him. Two years of a lot of trial and error and a lot of screaming and crying. The homework routine is far from perfection, but it is also far from daily afternoon combat over the day's tedious assignments. As the full extent of Ricochet's written expression disorder was revealed, our homework routine changed a bit, but for the better. Here are the tips we implemented into our homework routine that we used successfully until Ricochet started doing his homework on the computer:

Like Clockwork

I've experimented quite a bit with the time of day that we do homework. It was quickly apparent that waiting until after dinner (and after medications had worn off) was not going to work for Ricochet or for me. We then tried right after school at 3:30 PM and at 4 PM, which is about thirty minutes after we arrived home from school. I liked the idea of some free time for Ricochet to unwind and take a break from schoolwork that the 4 PM schedule offered. Many families find that successful; however, it just didn't work for Ricochet. In thirty minutes time he would become engrossed in something fun, and then it was a battle to get him to stop and do homework. I feel a little like ~~the wicked witch~~ a schoolmarm making him do homework the minute we get home from school pickup, but he does his best work at that time. He's been doing his homework when we get in from school so long now that it is habit — he comes in, puts his shoes and backpack away, and gets started on his homework, often without even being asked now.

Of course, we don't always come straight home from school. Sometimes I'm working and someone else picks him up. Sometimes we have afterschool appointments or just need to run to the grocery store. But Ricochet knows that we do homework when we return home from school, whatever time that may read on the clock. He has come to expect it, and that makes afternoons much more ~~tolerable~~ enjoyable for both of us.

I am lucky that my work schedule is somewhat flexible and I mostly work from home as it allows me to often pick up my kids from school and start homework by mid-afternoon. If you work typical office hours, consider what will be the best time of day for your child to do homework out of the times you have the opportunity to work together. If he's an early riser, he could complete homework in the mornings before school — if he can focus at that time of day and you can get up early, too. It could be that the best time for your family is when you finally arrive home for the day. Or maybe your child is in a structured afterschool program and can do their homework with assistance from program staff during that time. Experiment with the time and location that your child does homework until you find what works best for them; it will be different for each child. Be flexible about the when and where, too — if my son did his best homework underneath his bed at 6 AM, by golly I'd go with it. Homework is so hard for children with ADHD and learning disabilities, and they are working so much harder at school all day — who can blame them for being resistant to homework really?

Even Homework Needs a Home

Assign a particular spot in your house for homework papers and supplies, and keep them in the same spot. When I say, "Time to do homework," Ricochet immediately goes to his homework spot. Well, not immediately; even the best laid plan will not cure the typical resistance to homework. We keep Ricochet's homework folder, pencils, etc. on the end of the snack bar. We keep all possible required homework supplies there so he doesn't have the distraction of getting up to fetch something.

Now that Ricochet has some technological accommodations for dysgraphia and written expression disorder, he does his spelling homework and reading log on the computer. That eliminated the need for a homework corner with traditional supplies at our house. When it is homework time, he reads first, wherever he is comfortable. He can stand on his head on the sofa, for all I care, if that's what gets the reading done without battle! Then he comes to my desk to work on my computer. He's great with technology, and typing is so much easier for him than writing assignments by hand. This modification actually allowed me to stop standing over him constantly nagging during homework for the first time since he started school. That was certainly a welcome change!

If you don't have a timer or don't use one with your child with ADHD, I ~~demand~~ super-strongly recommend its implementation. My favorite is the Time Timer*, but any household timer will work. When the timer sounds at the end of Ricochet's thirty minutes for reading, he jumps up ~~in pure elation at being~~

finished, completes his reading log, and then puts the homework folder back in his backpack (with a little prodding and a lot of reminders).

Multiple Hours of Homework is Not Okay

Homework is designed to prove to a teacher that a child has mastered the subject matter, and it is also sometimes an exercise in repetition for knowledge retention. Every child in the class is given the same homework more often than not, regardless of their learning differences, unless there's already an established IEP or 504 Plan to the contrary. It's your duty as your child's advocate and #1 cheerleader to be sure the homework is appropriate in reference to their disabilities. Yes, this is open to discussion, either through teamwork with their classroom teacher or through a formal IEP or 504 Plan accommodation. Don't let anyone tell you all children must do the same volume of homework — they are wrong; I am right.

Doing three hours of homework when their peers are only spending one hour on it is essentially punishing your child for having a learning disability.

Teachers plan homework with a certain time frame in mind for how long students should spend on homework each day. Your child should only have to do homework as long as their classmates, even if that means they don't complete an equal volume of work. I hear parents of kids with ADHD and/ or learning disabilities complain all the time about the overwhelming number of hours it takes to complete homework every night. Doing three hours of homework when their peers are only spending one hour on it is essentially *punishing your child for having a learning disability.* Take a minute and really let that sink in. Write it down on a sticky note if you need to. Having your child spend twice or triple as much time on their homework is punishing them for having a disability, which is totally out of their control, ~~no matter what the ADHD haters say~~. That is not okay for you, and it's not okay for your child either. Always ask your child's teacher how long homework is meant to take their students, and let them know if it is taking your child a lot longer on a consistent basis. Ask for modified assignments to be part of their IEP or 504 Plan if it isn't offered at that time.

Also, scaling the amount of homework to your child's learning differences and special needs is a crucial element in the success of the homework routine and a safe-guard for your child's self-esteem. For example, in third grade, Ricochet read for fifteen minutes each day, while the master third grade homework structure at his school called for twenty minutes. There was a lot of resistance and inability to finish twenty minutes of reading, but fifteen minutes was just the right amount for Ricochet to stick to the task and not feel overwhelmed. While he is above grade level in reading, he was also allowed to have me read aloud to him if that's what it took to get the assignment finished. I have found that he often asks me to read to him just to have time together. I agree, but on the condition that we take turns reading aloud by alternating paragraphs. He usually ends up reading most of it himself anyway, just with me alongside him for moral support. As he gets older, he is using technology that reads books aloud to him and highlights the text in synch with the audio voice (Bookshare offers this).

Also, get creative and tailor homework to the way your child learns. Ricochet is a visual and tactile learner, so we make homework visual and hands-on as much as we can — it was a lot easier to do so in the earlier elementary grades. Use dried macaroni for math and even spelling. Recently, we used candy corn for ratio problems in math, and then he got to eat the candy (Yes! It had ~~those evil~~ artificial colors and flavors, but I was desperate and there was no time to search town for an all-natural version.) as a reward for finishing each problem.

Does your child love to paint? Let them paint their spelling words or their illustration for their writing assignments. Painting letters is actually a common occupational therapy tool for children that struggle with handwriting. What about play dough? I purchased a box of cookie cutters with the full alphabet and numbers 0-9 for play dough play when Ricochet was in first grade. You can do spelling and math with these and a can or two of play dough. It will take longer, but it makes homework more engaging and fun.

Most of Ricochet's teachers are perfectly content with our customization of the homework plan once they get to know him and his special learning requirements. I've modified his homework as needed myself for five years now — when he is old enough to get grades for homework {hold me!}, we will only need his teachers to comply with specific modifications as modified assignments is already an accommodation in his IEP.

Similar alterations can be made for middle school and high school homework, too. For instance, a student should be allowed to complete a percentage of the problems on a math worksheet (maybe every other problem) to show they have mastered the content when the entire assignment will take too long or is overwhelming. Shortening assignments will reduce their anxiety too, making it easier to work and study in the first place.

Instill Good Study Habits

Good study habits are even more crucial for children with ADHD and learning disabilities. There are some general ground rules that should always be followed:

> › TV and other distractions must be turned off during homework. However, music in the background helps some children focus and can be permissible. It is a distraction for me, but Ricochet and his sister both do homework better with music on, especially when listening

with headphones. Experiment with this and see what is best for your child.

> Praise and reward often (more often than would feel natural for a neurotypical child).

> Take breaks as needed. Who says you have to finish homework in one sitting? I just want to get it over with, but that's too much pressure for Ricochet. Allow your child to get up and stretch, get a snack, jump on the trampoline, etc. Just don't allow them any screen time during breaks because you won't likely get back to the homework amicably.

Most importantly, relax. It's just homework. Don't tell yourself that if your child's classmates have to do a certain amount of work, then your child should have to do it all, too. Don't think the only way your child will learn all the curriculum is by doing homework. And for goodness sakes, don't let homework ruin the few hours you have with your child each night. Some things are just more important.

REMAIN CALM CHECKLIST

Post this where it can serve as a reminder.

1. Recognize that what LOOKS LIKE WILLFUL disobedience MAY not be.

CRUCIAL!

2. Express empathy for their feelings.

3. Guide them through frustration.

4. Work together to PROBLEM SOLVE WHILE teaching them LAGGING SKILLS.

5. Remember who is really in control of the situation. You are!

CREATE A HOMEWORK TOOLKIT

Having all materials potentially needed to complete homework ready and in one place can possibly curb a lot of procrastination and distraction during homework. Make a homework toolkit or station that meets the individual needs of your child. Get creative!

☐ Pencils (Sharpened)

☐ Pencil Grips

☐ Extra Erasers

☐ Ink Pens

☐ Markers

☐ Colored Pencils (Sharpened)

☐ Highlighter

☐ Appropriate Scissors

☐ Notebook Paper

☐ Construction Paper and/or Blank Copy Paper

☐ Graph Paper

☐ Calculator

☐ Ruler

☐ Dictionary

☐ Index Cards

☐ Tape

☐ Glue Stick

☐ Post_it Notes

☐ Post_it Flags

☐ Charger for Tablet (if Regularly Used for Homework)

☐ Clipboard (if Not Working at a Table or Desktop)

☐ Anything Else Your Child May Use for Homework

Don't Forget Siblings

ADHD has a way of hijacking a family, especially when you are still working to find effective treatment and to get your bearings parenting a child with ADHD. Take a time out often to consider what the other children in your family experience at home and during family time.

> Do they hear a lot of yelling and/or threatening?

> Are they subjected to frequent arguments between parents about the best way to handle ADHD?

> Do they constantly have to listen to discussions about ADHD?

> Do they get time alone with you, or is all your time consumed by managing your child with ADHD?

I could check every one of those items off at one time or another. We still struggle a great deal with parental arguments over ADHD behaviors and discipline, even in front of the kids. (I need time in naughty corner myself!)

Reflect and *be honest* with yourself. Once you have a clear picture of what the siblings in your household are going through, multiply it by ten and you'll have an idea of how it *feels* to them. Pretty rotten, right?

It is so easy to get caught up in ADHD drama and let it consume your time. In fact, it's hard not to let ADHD control nearly all your moments. It's tough to find the balance for all our children when there's always a strong magnetism like ADHD demanding inequality in parenting. First, you have to talk with your other children honestly about why you must give more time to one child in your family. Depending on their age, they may not understand that rationally yet, but they still need to hear the truth. Then you have to carve out time for them, too — time when ADHD can't pull you away from giving them your undivided attention.

I first began to realize I was letting ADHD interrupt my relationship with Warrior Girl when she started fleeing the room every time Mr. T and I talked about (and often argued about) ADHD. I heard a lot of, "You would buy it for Ricochet," or, "You get him special stuff all the time that I don't get." But the toll ADHD was taking on my (mostly) neurotypical daughter came crashing down on me one day in family counseling.

Warrior Girl had scored high for anxiety a few weeks before, after we and her teachers completed some diagnostic rating scales. This particular day was her first counseling appointment purely about her. She was first asked to simply share all the things that had been bothering her. I was shushed by our counselor several times when I tried to speak up and defend myself against Warrior Girl's accusations. It was good to let her express exactly how she *felt* though, and it was advantageous for me to hear her out. I struggled not to defend my parenting at every over-dramatic story she told.

"They might as well build an altar in our house with statues of Ricochet to bow down to and worship him," she offered at one point, very matter-of-fact and quite serious.

I was stunned.

I had held my tongue up to that point at the counselor's urging, but as soon as the suggestion was made that we "worship" Ricochet, a wounded "Oh, come on!" escaped my lips. That accusation hurt a lot — it hurt my parent pride, but it also hurt my heart for her.

Oh, the drama of a tween girl! That statement was surely overdramatic, but it was enlightening to know what she was truly feeling nonetheless, even if her feelings were irrational.

Warrior Girl was given an official diagnosis of general anxiety disorder that day, not due to her feelings of inequity with her brother, but because of some significant social issues and separation anxiety she was experiencing. I didn't feel like she needed a "diagnosis" and I didn't want another kid with a disorder, frankly. In fact, it was very hard for me to accept a diagnosis for her, and I found myself trying to talk her counselor down to just social anxiety disorder because somehow that one seemed easier to accept.

The funny thing is, I see so much of myself in Warrior Girl. I had a very hard time with going anyplace where I didn't know anyone. What am I saying? "Had"? I still get physically nervous in these situations. There are many things I'd like to participate in that I don't just for this reason. I made a lot of poor decisions as a teen and young adult working for peer acceptance and trying to fit in. I really don't want to see Warrior Girl go down that path, too. I suppose I would be diagnosed with an anxiety disorder too, if I asked. Heck, we all probably fall under the parameters of one thing or another.

Our counselor gave Warrior Girl and me two assignments that day:

1. Warrior Girl was to daily write in a journal all the things that she worried about that day and bring it back to counseling with her.

2. I was tasked with planning and executing activities just for Warrior Girl and me — no boys and no ADHD allowed. The following weekend, she and I went to our favorite bakery for coffee, chocolate cake, and light-hearted conversation.

You may think Warrior Girl's admissions to our counselor were over-dramatic, too — but ask yourself if your other children might be *feeling* the same way, even if their feelings are far from reality. It is crucial for you to take time to delve deeply into the possibility that your other children may be feeling neglected and unloved. No parent wants to hear that or accept that, but you have to acknowledge it for the wellbeing of those other children.

Here are some things you can do to try to rebalance your parenting scales:

› Ask your other children to be candid with you and tell you how they are feeling. Don't correct them if they exaggerate; that's your peephole into how they really feel.

› Be sure to praise your other children often, even if you don't think it's as necessary for them as it is for your child with ADHD. Children want to see equality in your love for them, and they measure it in all sorts of inappropriate ways.

› Schedule time for the siblings and each parent. Take them to do something they love and that they don't get to do when their sibling with ADHD is around. Try to have these activities twice a month or more.

› Include the entire family in counseling.

› Ask your children without ADHD to keep a journal of how they are feeling. They don't necessarily have to let you read it — just expressing their feelings can be therapeutic.

› Reward them just because you love them sometimes.

ADHD is hard on your entire tribe, not just the individual with ADHD. Be sure you remember and acknowledge this and work on balancing the scales as much as possible. The feelings and self-esteem of every one of your children are fragile.

Step 9: Start Enjoying Your Child

❯❯❯❯❯❯❯❯❯❯❯

"We worry about what a child will become tomorrow, yet we forget that he is someone today."

~Stacia Tauscher

See Your Child, Not Their ADHD

I do not have an "ADHD child," and neither do you. We have a "child with ADHD," "a child who has ADHD," or the like, but no one has an "ADHD child." You probably think I've lost my marbles right about now, but I'll explain the enormity of the difference simply rearranging the order of the words makes in just a moment.

It's not accurate to say "my child is ADHD" either. Oh, I hate that one! My child isn't ADHD, and I'm certain the same is true for your child. ADHD doesn't define who my son is — it is only one part of him, and a small part of all that defines him at that. Does it feel like ADHD defines him at times? Yes! Sure it does. I'd be kidding myself if I didn't acknowledge that. But there is so much more than ADHD to Ricochet, and so much more that makes up every child who has ADHD.

Just by carefully choosing your words and the order of their phrasing, you can reduce your child's sense that they are defined by their ADHD. It's a simple change that seems innocuous, but its effects are huge.

As much as Ricochet struggles in school, he feels like ADHD is his defining trait — the #1 thing about him — because it's there all the time. Our counselor recently decided to do an activity with Ricochet to show what a small part of him ADHD actually is. They traced his outline on a giant piece of paper, labeled all the parts of his being, and then talked about the amount of wonderful other things about him that have nothing to do with ADHD. He emerged from her office beaming that day.

I encourage you to do this activity with your kids with ADHD (or any other disability) as well. It is a powerful visual to help these special kids begin to overcome the feeling that their life is ruined by ADHD. That is enormously valuable!

My child, who happens to have ADHD and learning disabilities, is smart, kind-hearted, gifted, funny, handsome, a whiz with electronics, great at math and science, a loyal friend, has an infectious smile, loves Legos and RC cars, and so much more. He is a great kid who happens to also struggle with ADHD.

Take a few moments and review the list of all the positive qualities of your child you made back in *Step 1: Get Over It*. Add any more things you think of now. Make a conscious effort to focus on these wonderful traits often. Reframing your thoughts is a powerful tool — you'll find that you focus on the ADHD less and less as time goes by and as your child grows up.

I found that reframing my thinking by simply refusing to call Ricochet an "ADHD child" any longer created a sharper focus on his wonderfulness and keeps me more positive and optimistic more often. That, in and of itself, is a magnificent gift.

Focus on the Positive

There are so many things in this world that can drag us down if we let them. ADHD is certainly on that list for all individuals who have it, and their families. Constantly thinking about ADHD creates a perpetual stream of negativity. Don't get me wrong, ADHD is pervasive and it's hard not to think about it. When your child is first diagnosed, you won't think about much else. It does get easier to push it toward the back of your mind as time goes on though — I promise.

When Ricochet was first diagnosed with ADHD in November, 2008, I couldn't think about anything else. By that time I had already been researching learning disabilities and trying to figure out what was preventing his school success. I was already a momma on a mission for sure. The diagnosis merely gave me a concrete direction for all that focused energy.

For two years, I spent little time on anything else. The simple day-to-day got done, but I pushed aside everything I could to spend as much time as possible researching ADHD. I was obsessed because I was certain there was something that was going to "fix" my child's problems. I knew there wasn't a cure, but I was still honed in on fixing it, and that can't happen either.

The more I obsessed over ADHD, the more I perseverated on it. The only conversations I had with Mr. T were about ADHD, even in front of our children. The only thing anyone who knew me well heard me talk about was ADHD. I realize now how off-putting it was, but I was compelled by fear and desperation at the time.

I'm not sure of the trigger, but at some point I accepted that ADHD, and some negative repercussions, were here to stay. Honestly, I probably got tired of thinking about it, hoping for change, then feeling like a failure. I was stuck in the muck of disappointment so often back then. Finally, I came up for air to recognize the pattern and that this is one thing this momma can't fix.

That acceptance lifted an enormous weight. It opened up so much room to focus on other things about my son, such as his interests in Boy Scouts and woodworking. When I stopped focusing on all the negative traits, I could finally see the many wonderful parts of my son they were obscuring. Then I had the time and energy to focus on his talents and interests.

The shift in our family when I finally gained traction on the learning curve of parenting a child with ADHD was palpable — it was as if we let out one harmonious sigh of relief. Are our days now filled with hunky-dory dancing and cheer? *Uh, no* — I didn't say our fairy godmother visited and waved her magic wand over us now, did I? If you see her, tell her we're happy to oblige that though. Of course there are still struggles! The difference is that now we don't let those struggles guide us and define us. Optimism and joy feel so much better than fear and helplessness.

Nurture their Gifts

You have made a list of all the wonderfulness that is your child, who happens to also have ADHD. You've decided to stop trying to fix their ADHD and focus your energy on their positive traits and interests instead. These are giant steps in and of themselves. Now it's time to use that knowledge to create a happier and healthier child by nurturing their gifts.

To start with, choose a couple of things on your list that your child is most interested in or enthusiastic about. How can you nurture these talents or interests? If he is interested in chemistry, sign him up for chemistry camp, or get a book of home chemistry projects and work on them together. If he loves baseball, sign him up for Little League. If he likes to read a lot, be sure you go to the library once or twice a week so he always has something new to read. If he is a talented illustrator, get him into some art classes and make sure he has the supplies he needs to grow in his talent. There are endless possibilities here. The key is to make opportunities available in the areas of your child's interest.

Don't be afraid of failure. It's hard to find a good fit for our kids with ADHD sometimes, but the only way to know if it will work out or not is to try. I read consistently that baseball and other team sports are not a good fit for kids with ADHD. It definitely wasn't a good fit for my hyperactive, clinically-inattentive kid! But I know for a fact there are some talented Major League Baseball players who have ADHD and are living their dream. What if their parents had decided not to try baseball when they were young because they knew the game could be difficult for those with ADHD? Sounds tragic, huh? Failure is a part of life. I realize it is a larger part of life for kids with ADHD, but we learn from every experience and adjust accordingly. If they are interested in something, give it a go.

This Too Shall Pass

Kids grow up and mature, even our kids with ADHD. Not at the "typical" rate for their chronological age, but they do mature and catch up somewhat in early adulthood usually. As these super-special

> *Parenting a child with ADHD doesn't have to be a constant struggle for hope and a frequent sequestration in a pit of helpless despair.*

kids of ours get older, life with a child with ADHD usually gets easier — not easy, but easi**ER**. ADHD is not going away. (This is hotly debated; I think it's actually "going away" for some in adulthood, but those individuals had a milder ADHD and learned to cope and compensate very well.) But life with ADHD gets simpler, and the daily excessive difficulties will pass, for the most part.

Around Ricochet's ninth birthday, I distinctly noticed that he was more self-aware, attempting to regulate his behavior sometimes, and that we were all learning how to cope with and actually live life despite his ADHD. It took us nearly three years after diagnosis and the beginning of treatment to reach that point. Three years is a long time to struggle multiple times every day — but I had to research this thing called ADHD and what it means about my child, how to manage it, and how to get the school to help him. No one explained to me how to get to know my child in a meaningful way as it relates to ADHD. No one told us how to work with the school and secure educational help for Ricochet. No one explained meltdowns to me and how to identify triggers to nip them in the bud. And certainly, no one told me parenting a child with ADHD doesn't have to be a constant struggle for hope and a frequent sequestration in a pit of helpless despair.

I know all these things now though, and I can't express how much I wish I had known them when Ricochet was diagnosed. That's why I wrote this book for you — I don't want to see parents of children with ADHD struggle as much as I did, nor for as long as I did.

There's no over-arching manual for parenting. I am lucky that I had a great example in my own family growing up. I know mother's intuition is a powerful force, and I continue to envision my children as healthy, happy, successful adults to cement the goal. Now we have to work on it, learn from our mistakes, adjust our performance, take coaching from others, and celebrate each small victory as we would a home run.

Those small victories overcome the little failures and add up to a game well-played and won.

Stay strong. Love that special child of yours with all your might. Work *with* your child to minimize the hold their weaknesses have on them and increase the positive moments in their life. And, most importantly, don't let ADHD control your family — take control of ADHD and live. Really enjoy living! If you work at it, you can create joy in your special parenthood.

Good luck, my fellow Warrior Parent!

Appendix

Resources We've Found Useful

Visit bit.ly/ADHDresources for direct links to these, and many more, resources.

> HowdaHug

> Planet Box

> AdditudeMag.com

> ADDconnect.com

> LivesInTheBalance.org

> LD.org

> LDonline.com

> Chewable Pencil Toppers

> Weighted Blankets

> Skweezers Bed Sheets and Body Socks

> Case-It Velcro Closure Binders

> The Zones of Regulation

> SpecialEducationAdvisor.com

> EasytoLovebut.com

> aMomsViewofADHD.com

> Immersion Reading on Kindle Fire

> ADDYteen.com

> ToysAreTools.com

> Bookshare.org

> TherapyShoppe.com

> Happy Mama Conference & Retreat

> ImpactADHD.com

> WrightsLaw.com

Glossary of Special Education Terms

The following glossary was provided by Robert M. Tudisco, Attorney, Non-Profit Consultant & Motivational Speaker. Learn more about Mr. Tudisco and his services at www.RobertTudisco.com.

504 Plan - A plan setting forth services and/or special accommodations for a child with a disability, pursuant to Section 504 of the Rehabilitation Act of Counterpart of an Individualized Education Plan (IEP) under the Individuals with Disabilities Education Act (IDEA).

Americans with Disabilities Act (ADA) - A federal anti-discrimination statute that defines which organizations are required to provide access to those with disabilities. It can be used to protect students with disabilities from discrimination for individuals whose disability substantially impacts a major life activity (i.e., education).

Assistive Technology - An external device or functionality that seeks to remediate a learning disability, or other disorder, or to provide equal access to educational services to children with disabilities.

Attention Deficit/ Hyperactivity Disorder (AD/HD) - This general term encompasses Attention Deficit Disorder (ADD), hyperactive, inattentive, or combined types.

Behavior Intervention Plan (BIP) - A plan of positive behavioral interventions, made a part of the IEP of a child whose behaviors interfere with that child's learning or their peers.

Code of Federal Regulations (CFR) - Set of administrative regulations established by the United States Department of Education to interpret IDEA.

Committee for Special Education (CSE) - Sometimes referred to as the special education team that is required by the Individuals with Disabilities Education Act (IDEA) to provide an Individualized Education Program (IEP) to address the needs of children from kindergarten through high school graduation, or the age of 21, who qualify for special education services pursuant to the statute.

Committee for Preschool Special Education (CPSE) - Similar in operation to the Committee for Special Education, but deals with children from two years of age up to Kindergarten.

Co-Morbid or Co-Occurring Disorder - A disorder, or Specific Learning Disability (SLA) that is present along with another functional disability.

DSM - Diagnostic and Statistical Manual of Mental Disorders published by the American Psychiatric Association. It is the main diagnostic reference for mental health professionals in the United States.

Due Process Hearing (Impartial Due Process Hearing) - An impartial hearing which commences upon a formal request by either parents or LEA. The hearing is conducted before an Independent Hearing Officer (IHO) or Administrative Law Judge (ALJ) who takes testimony under oath and presides. The hearing is stenographically or tape recorded and a written decision is required to resolve the dispute between the parties. Either party can appeal the decision of an IHO to a State Review Officer (SRO).

Family Educational Rights and Privacy Act (FERPA) - Federal statute that ensures both the right to privacy and access of a student's educational records. It is important to note that the protection of this law for children under 18 belongs to the parent and/or legal guardian, while that protection switches to the child at age 18; subject to a few limited exceptions, schools and parents must obtain written consent of the student to share educational information.

Free Appropriate Public Education (FAPE) - The right of all (K-12) students with disabilities guaranteed by Section 504 of the Rehabilitation Act of 1973 and the Individuals with Disabilities Education Improvement Act (IDEA). This requires public schools to provide appropriate services, at no cost to the student or their family, which will ensure access to an education that is equal to students without disabilities.

Independent Hearing Officer (IHO) - An officer appointed by a State Department of Education to hear disputes between parents and school districts at a Due Process hearing. Depending upon the testimonial record, an IHO has the authority to subpoena documents and/or order either side to comply with his or her directive.

Independent Educational Evaluation (IEE) - In the event that a student's parents do not agree with the educational evaluation conducted by the school district, parents have the right to request an independent evaluation of their child at no cost to them. This should not be confused with a private educational evaluation that parents should always consider conducting themselves, if they can afford to do so.

Individuals with Disabilities Education Improvement Act (IDEA) - An educational statute enacted by the Federal government and codified under 20 U.S.C 1400. IDEA governs children up to the age of 21 or up to achieving their high school diploma. The statute, now referred to as the Individuals with Disabilities Education Improvement Act, ensures that children with qualifying disabilities receive a Free Appropriate Public Education (FAPE).

Individual Education Plan (IEP) - An education program required by the Individuals with Disabilities Education Improvement Act, to be designed to meet the specific needs of a disabled child who qualifies for special education. The IEP must contain annual goals and be reviewed on an annual basis.

Learning Disability (LD) or Specific Learning Disability (SLD) - A disability category under IDEA, which includes disorders that affect the ability to understand and/or use spoken or written language, or which may be manifested by difficulties with listening, thinking, speaking, reading, writing, spelling, and/or performing mathematical calculations. LD or SLD also includes minimal brain dysfunction (AD/HD), dyslexia, dysgraphia developmental aphasia, and other disorders.

Least Restrictive Environment (LRE) - A requirement under IDEA, that special education and/or related services be provided in, or as close to, a mainstream environment as is possible or practical under the circumstances.

Local Educational Agency (LEA) - The local school district responsible for providing services to a student or group of students.

Mediation - A procedural safeguard under IDEA to resolve disputes between parents and LEAs. Mediation is a voluntary alternative to a to a due process hearing and may not be used to deny or delay a due process hearing. The mediation must be conducted by a qualified and impartial mediator who is trained in effective mediation techniques. The decision of the mediator is non-binding, and a disagreement between the parties can still be the basis for a due process hearing.

Obsessive Compulsive Disorder (OCD) - is classified in DSM IV as an anxiety disorder characterized by distressing intrusive thoughts and/or repetitive actions that interfere with the individual's daily functioning.

Occupational Therapy (OT) - is a related service used to remediate deficits or developmental problems with sensory integration and fine motor skills.

Oppositional Defiant Disorder (ODD) - refers to a recurrent pattern of negative, defiant, disobedient, and hostile behavior toward authority figures lasting at least six months.

Response to Intervention (RTI) – is a general education pre-referral process to help children who are having difficulty learning and achieving at grade level. It was designed to provide additional support to students without having to go through the special education evaluation process. However, RTI may not be used to delay the evaluation process and can be implemented during that process.

Section 504 of the Rehabilitation Act of 1973 (504) - A civil rights statute prohibiting agencies set forth in the Americans with Disabilities Act (ADA) from discriminating against individuals on the basis of their disability.

State Review Officer (SRO) - An officer appointed by the State to review the decision, on appeal, of an Independent Hearing Officer (IHO) after a Due Process Hearing.

Thank You for Reading!

Dear Reader,

I hope you enjoyed *What to Expect When Parenting a Child with ADHD*. Writing this book has given purpose to my son's ADHD and my journey parenting a child with ADHD. For updates on my special boy for many years to come, follow my blog at BoyWithoutInstructions.com, and follow me on Facebook at Facebook.com/PennyWilliamsAuthor. As well, visit WhatToExpectADHD.com for links to all the resources mentioned in this book, and many more useful resources on parenting a child with ADHD.

I receive numerous emails from readers thanking me for sharing our journey and compiling ADHD resources. As an author, I love feedback, so that is very rewarding. You and your family are the reason I will continue to write about ADHD. So, tell me what you liked, what you loved, and even what you hated about this book. I would truly love to hear from you. Write to me at penny@pennywilliamsauthor.com and visit me online at PennyWilliamsAuthor.com.

I need to ask a favor, too. I'd love a review of *What to Expect When Parenting a Child with ADHD*. Positive or negative, I need your feedback. Reviews are tough to come by, but they can make or break the success of a book and its author. If you can spare just five minutes, please visit the *What to Expect When Parenting a Child with ADHD* pages on Amazon.com and Goodreads.com and submit your candid review.

Thank you for reading *What to Expect When Parenting a Child with ADHD*. Look for my previous book, *Boy Without Instructions: Surviving the Learning Curve of Parenting a Child with ADHD*, available on Amazon and BarnesandNoble.com now.

With sincerest gratitude,

Penny

Purchase Other Titles by Penny Williams

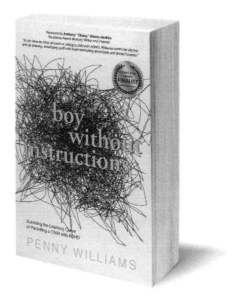

Most books on ADHD don't dare expose the genuine grit of the moment-by-moment peaks and valleys of this special parenthood — the gut-wrenching, crying on the bathroom floor, feeling like you're losing your mind truth of the matter that is learning to successfully parent a child with ADHD. *Boy Without Instructions* changes that.

Williams shares her unfiltered thoughts and emotions during her progression through this learning curve during this harrowing ride. Right before your eyes, this initially grief-stricken momma transforms from obsessed-with-ADHD control-freak and helicopter mom to optimistic and (mostly) confident parent of a child who happens to have ADHD. *Boy Without Instructions* validates your grief and guilt, yet reveals that it's truly possible to craft a (mostly) joy-filled life for your child with ADHD, yourself, and your family.

Purchase *Boy Without Instructions* on Amazon.com, BarnesandNoble.com, and through other select retailers.

Endnotes

1. Hallowell, Edward, MD and Jensen, Peter S., MD. Adapted from "Superparenting for ADD: An Innovative Approach to Raising Your Distracted Child," Ballantine, 2008.

2. American Academy of Pediatrics. Subcommittee on Attention-Deficit/ Hyperactivity Disorder and Committee on Quality Improvement. Clinical practice guideline: treatment of the school-aged child with attention-deficit/ hyperactivity disorder. Pediatrics. 2001;108(4):1033–1044.

3. "ADHD, Central Auditory Processing Disorder, & Learning Disabilities."ADDtreatmentcenter.com. N.p., 2005. Web. 4 Sept. 2014.

4. "Information About ADHD ADHD Coaching FAQs." ADHD Coaching FAQs. Edge Foundation, n.d. Web. 05 Sept. 2014.

5. "Treatment." Centers for Disease Control and Prevention. Centers for Disease Control and Prevention, 20 Aug. 2014. Web. 05 Sept. 2014.

6. Faber Taylor, A. and Kuo, F. E. (2011), Could Exposure to Everyday Green Spaces Help Treat ADHD? Evidence from Children's Play Settings. Applied Psychology: Health and Well-Being, 3: 281–303. doi: 10.1111/j.1758-0854.2011.01052.x

7. Pontifex, Matthew B., Brian J. Saliba, Lauren B. Raine, Daniel L. Picchietti, and Charles H. Hillman. "Exercise Improves Behavioral, Neurocognitive, and Scholastic Performance in Children with Attention-Deficit/Hyperactivity Disorder." The Journal of Pediatrics162.3 (2013): 543-51. Web.

8. Biel, Lindsey, and Nancy K. Peske. Raising a Sensory Smart Child: The Definitive Handbook for Helping Your Child with Sensory Processing Issues. New York, NY: Penguin, 2009. Print.

9. Dodson, William W., MD. "Rejection Sensitive Dysphoria." Dodson ADHD Center. N.p., n.d. Web. 05 Sept. 2014.

10. Faber Taylor, A. and Kuo, F. E. (2011), Could Exposure to Everyday Green Spaces Help Treat ADHD? Evidence from Children's Play Settings. Applied Psychology: Health and Well-Being, 3: 281–303. doi: 10.1111/j.1758-0854.2011.01052.x

11. Bosch, Laurentine Ten. "Top 10 Food Additives to Avoid." Food Matters. N.p., 23 Nov. 2010. Web. 05 Sept. 2014.

12. Kim, Susanna. "11 Food Ingredients Banned Outside the U.S. That We Eat."ABC News. ABC News Network, n.d. Web. 05 Sept. 2014.

13. Kobylewski, Sarah, and Michael F. Jacobson, PhD. "Food Dyes: A Rainbow of Risks." Food Dyes (n.d.): n. pag. Center for Science in the Public Interest, June 2012. Web. 5 Sept. 2014.

14. Editors of PureHealthMD. ""Dangers of Food Additives"" HowStuffWorks. N.p., n.d. Web. 05 Sept. 2014.

15. Maryse F. Bouchard, David C. Bellinger, Robert O. Wright, and Marc G. Weisskopf. "Attention-Deficit/Hyperactivity Disorder and Urinary Metabolites of Organophosphate Pesticides." Pediatrics peds.2009-3058; published ahead of print May 17, 2010,doi:10.1542/peds.2009-3058

16. Individuals with Disabilities Education Act, 20 U.S.C. § 1400, et. seq Part B

17. http://www2.ed.gov/policy/speced/guid/idea/letters/2007-4/redact112807eligibility4q2007.pdf

18. ED Memorandum to State Directors of Special Education, 2011

19. National Dissemination Center for Children with Disabilities (NICHCY), Publication: Questions Often Asked by Parents, April 2009

20. National Alliance on Mental Health, http://www.nami.org/Template.cfm?Section=By_Illness&Template=/TaggedPage/TaggedPageDisplay.cfm&TPLID=54&ContentID=23047

21. Mann, Denise. "Minimize School Morning Mayhem for Children With ADHD." WebMD. WebMD, n.d. Web. 06 Sept. 2014.

44971936R00162

Made in the USA
San Bernardino, CA
28 January 2017